Vermont
Covered
Bridges
by
Harold Stiver

Vermont Covered Bridges
A Guide for Photographers and Explorers

Published by Harold Stiver

License Notes

Version 2.0
ISBN #978-0-9868670-5-7

For Emily and Kelly, Best Daughters Ever

Table of Contents

Windsor County   **Page 118**
Best's Covered Bridge, Bower's Covered Bridge, Windsor-Cornish Covered Bridge, Martinsville Covered Bridge, Willard Covered Bridge, Willard Twin Covered Bridge, Baltimore Covered Bridge, Upper Falls Covered Bridge, Salmond Covered Bridge, Titcomb Covered Bridge, Middle Covered Bridge, Lincoln Covered Bridge, Taftsville Covered Bridge, South Pomfret Covered Bridge

How to use this Book

For each of the 103 historical or Traditional Covered Bridges remaining in Vermont, we have included photographs as well as descriptive and statistical data. Traditional Covered Bridges are those that follow the building practices of the Nineteenth Century and the early part of the Twentieth Century or those built later that follow those methods. All of these bridges have had repairs done as portions wear out, and some may have been almost entirely replaced through the years. I have used "The National Society for the Preservation of Covered Bridges, Inc." list of what they consider as Traditional Bridges.

Following is data included for each bridge

Name: This is listed in bold type, and where there are other names, it is the common name or the name listed on an accompanying plaque.

Other Names: Underneath the Common Name in brackets, you will find other names that the bridge has been known by.

Nearest Town and **County** are listed.

It is frustrating to go on an excursion to see something and not be able to find it. This book offers you multiple ways to ensure that doesn't happen.

GPS Position: This is our recommended method. Enter the coordinates in a good GPS unit and it should take you right there. You, of course, must use care that you are not led off road or on a dangerous route. In particular be careful you are not led onto a non-maintained road in the winter.

Detailed Driving Directions: Directions from a town near to the bridge.

Builder: If known, the name of the original builder(s) is listed.

Year Built: As well as the year built, if it has been moved it will shown with the year preceded by the letter M and, if a major repair has been done, the year will be shown preceded by the letter R.

Truss Type: The type for the particular bridge will be listed. If you are interested in more information on the various types of trusses, access "Truss Types" from the Table of Contents.

Dimensions: The length and number of spans.

Photo Tips: We try to give you some idea of what opportunities you have as well as restrictions, and special items you may want to incorporate into the picture. You may also find some useful ideas from reading "Photographing Covered Bridges" from the Table of Contents.

Notes: A place where you can find additional items of interest about the bridge.

World Index Number:
Covered bridges are assigned a number to keep track of them which consists of three numbers separated by hyphens.

The first number represents the number of the U.S. State in alphabetical order. Following number 50 for the 50th state are additional numbers for Canadian provinces. Thus the numbers 05 represents California.

The second set of numbers represents the county of that state, again based on alphabetical order. Humboldt is the 12th county alphabetically in California, and it is designated as 05-12.

Each bridge in that county is given a number as it was discovered or built. Zane's Ranch was the fifth bridge discovered or built in the County of Humboldt, California and it therefore has the designation of 05-12-05. Sometimes you will see the first set of numbers replaced by the abbreviation for the state, thus CA-12-05.

A bridge is sometimes substantially rebuilt or replaced and it then has the suffix #2 added to it.

National Register of Historic Places: If the bridge has been registered, the date is given.

Photographing Covered Bridges

Some standard positions

Portal: Taken to show the ends of bridge or bridge opening. This view, usually symmetrical, will include various signs posted. This is also a good way to get run over, so be careful!

3/4 view: Shows both the front and sides of the bridge, and is often the most attractive.

Side view: Taken from a bank or from the river, this gives not only a nice view of the bridge but usually allows for some interesting foreground elements.

Interior view: An image taken from the interior of the bridge will show some interesting structure but there is not a lot of available light. A tripod is important and HDR processing is helpful.

Landscape View: With the bridge smaller in the frame, you can introduce the habitat around it, particularly effective with colorful autumn foliage.

Using HDR(High Dynamic Range)

HDR is a process where multiple images of varying exposure are combined to make one image.

It has a bad name with some people because many HDR images are super-saturated, a kind of digital age version of an Elvis painted on velvet. However, the process is actually about getting a full range of exposure with no burnt out highlights or blocked shadows. This is an ideal processing solution for photographing Covered Bridges where you often have open light sky set against dark shadowed landscape and structure.

I use a series of three exposures at levels of -1 2/3, 0, +1 2/3, and this normally runs the full exposure range encountered. It is important to use a stable tripod.

One situation where you may need a larger series is shooting from within a bridge and using the window to frame an outside scene. The dynamic range is huge and you will need to have a series with a much larger range.

There are a number of software programs you can use to combine these images including newer editions of Photoshop. I use Photomatix which I have found very versatile and easy to use.

Best times for photographing bridges

Mornings and evenings are generally the best times for outdoor photography but the use of HDR processing makes it easier even in bright direct light. Although any season is good for bridge photography including the winter, fall foliage included in a scene can be spectacular.

A Short History of Covered Bridges

Let's deal with that often posed question; "Why were the bridges covered"

1. Crossing animals thought it was a barn and entered easily. I like this suggestion, it shows imagination. However, its not the answer although the original bridges normally had no windows and this is said to be because animals would not be spooked by the sight of the water.

2. To cover up the unsightly truss structure. I don't think those early pioneers were that sensitive, and personally, I like the look of the trusses.

3. To keep snow off the traveled portion. In fact the bridge owners often paid to have the insides "snowed" in order to facilitate sleighs.

4. It offered some privacy to courting couples, hence "kissing bridges". That is a nice romantic notion but no.

In fact, the bridge was covered for economic reasons. The truss system was where much of the bridge's cost was found, and if left open to the elements, it deteriorated and the bridge became unstable and unsafe. Covering it protected this valuable portion and the roof could be replaced as needed with inexpensive materials and unskilled labor.

Without coverings, a bridge might only have a life span of a decade while one that was covered often lasted 75 years or more before repairs became necessary. Besides extending the longevity of a bridge, wooden covered bridges had the virtue that they could be constructed of local materials and there were many available workers skilled in working with wood.

The first known Covered Bridge in North America was built in 1804 by Theodore Burr. It was called the Waterford bridge and it spanned the Hudson River in New York.

For the rest of the century and into the 20th Century, Covered bridge building boomed as the country became populated and people needed to travel between communities. The cost of constructing and maintaining a bridge was normally borne by the nearby community and many bridges charged a toll as a method of offsetting these costs. The period from 1825 to 1875 was the heyday of bridge building but near the end of that period iron bridges began to supplant them.

The number of Covered bridges may have numbered 10,000 but have now dropped to about 950 spread throughout North America. Many have Historical Designations which provides them protection and many communities are interested in protecting their local historical bridges.

Addison County

Salisbury Station Covered Bridge

Township: Cornwall-Salisbury
County: Addison

GPS Position: N 43° 55.080' W 73° 10.445'
Directions: From the town of Cornwall go south on VT-30 for 3.2 miles and turn left on Swamp Road. The bridge is about 1.3 miles.

Crosses: Otter Creek
Carries: Swamp Road

Builder: Not known
Year Built: 1865 (R1969) (R1992) (R2002)
Truss Type: Town
Dimensions: Originally 1 Span but a center pier added 1969, 155 Feet

Photo Tip: Open front and sides.
Notes: Before the addition of the center pier in 1969, this was the longest single span covered bridge in Vermont.
World Index Number: 45-01-01
National Register of Historic Places: September 10, 1974

Spade Farm Covered Bridge
(Old Hollow Covered Bridge)

Township: Ferrisburgh
County: Addison

GPS Position: N 44° 12.415' W 73° 14.885'
Directions: From the town of North Ferrisburg go west on Old
Hollow Road and turn left on US-7 after 0.7 miles. The bridge is on the
west side of the road after 1.3 miles.

Crosses: Pond
Carries: Pedestrian walkway

Builder: Justin Miller
Year Built: 1850s (M1958) (R1999) (R2003)
Truss Type: Town
Dimensions: 1 Span, 85 Feet

Photo Tip: Easy from all sides. It has some interesting things inside it.
Notes: Originally located on Lewis Creek in North Ferrisburg,
Vermont, it was moved to its present location in 1958. While it is on
private property, visitors are allowed. While a sign on it indicates it was
built in 1824, research indicates it was more likely in the 1850s.

World Index Number: 45-01-02
National Register of Historic Places: Not listed

Halpin Covered Bridge
(High Covered Bridge)

Township: Middlebury-New Haven
County: Addison

GPS Position: N 44° 03.002' W 73° 08.459'
Directions: From the town of New Haven, go south on US-7/ Ethan Allen Highway and, after 4.7 miles, turn left on River Rd. After a mile, turn right on Halpin Rd. and then left on Halpin Covered Bridge Road. The bridge site is about 0.3 miles.

Crosses: New Haven River
Carries: Halpin Covered Bridge Road

Builder: Not known
Year Built: 1840
Truss Type: Town
Dimensions: 1 Span, 66 Feet

Photo Tip: Easy front and 3/4 view but a side view is a bit dodgy due to the height of the gorge.
Notes: At 41 feet, this is Vermont's highest bridge over it's water course. It is also one of the oldest. It was built to allow access to a marble quarry and the original abutments were made of marble.

World Index Number: 45-01-03
National Register of Historic Places: September 10, 1974

Pulp Mill Covered Bridge
(Paper Mill Covered Bridge)

Township: Middlebury-Weybridge
County: Addison

GPS Position: N 44° 01.453' W 73° 10.663'
Directions: From the town of Middlebury take Elm St east off US-7 for 0.2 miles and turn right on Seymour St. After 0.6 miles continue left onto Pulp Mill Bridge Road where you will find the bridge.

Crosses: Otter Creek
Carries: Pulp Mill Bridge Road

Builder: Not known
Year Built: 1853-1854
Truss Type: Multiple King with Burr Arch
Dimensions: Two additional pier supports were added in 1980, 199 Feet

Photo Tip: There is a side view near the dam side on the west side. Be careful
Notes: It is sometimes called Vermont's oldest covered bridges with build date c1820 but the World Guide to Covered Bridges lists it as 1853-1854.It is one of a few two lane bridges in North America which still carries vehicle traffic and it also has a pedestrian walkway.

World Index Number: 45-01-04
National Register of Historic Places: September 10, 1974

East Shoreham Railroad Covered Bridge
(Rutland Railroad Covered Bridge)

Township: Shoreham
County: Addison

GPS Position: N 43° 51.561' W 73° 15.363'
Directions: From the village of Shoreham go south on VT-22A for 0.5 miles and take the 1st left onto Richville Rd. After 3.2 miles turn right on Shoreham Depot Road and the parking lot for the bridge is 0.9 miles.

Crosses: Lemon Fair River
Carries: Abandoned rail line

Builder: Rutland Railroad Company
Year Built: 1897 (R1983)
Truss Type: Howe
Dimensions: 1 Span, 109 Feet

Photo Tip: The portal image as you approach gives a good idea of the size and will include some of the remaining tracks. The inside is also interesting but use a tripod.
Notes: One of two covered railroad bridges surviving in Vermont, this is a wonderful structure which ceased rail traffic in 1951. Due to the much heavier loads they carried, the railway bridges were more massively built and this is no exception.

World Index Number: 45-01-05
National Register of Historic Places: June 13, 1974

Bennington County

Bridge At The Green Covered Bridge
(Arlington Covered Bridge)

Township: Arlington
County: Bennington

GPS Position: N 43° 06.272' W 73° 13.208'
Directions: From the town of West Arlington, the bridge is off VT-313/ Batten Kill Rd on Covered Bridge Rd.

Crosses: Batten Kill
Carries: Covered Bridge Rd.

Builder: Not known
Year Built: 1852 (R1980) (R19982) (R2012)
Truss Type: Town
Dimensions:1 Span, 80 Feet

Photo Tip: Good views from all sides.
Notes: Found at the entrance to the Norman Rockwell homestead, it is a pleasant place for a family outing or picnic. In January 2012 there were repairs being made from the effects of Hurricane Irene as you can see in the image.

World Index Number: 45-02-01
National Register of Historic Places: August 28, 1973

Henry Covered Bridge

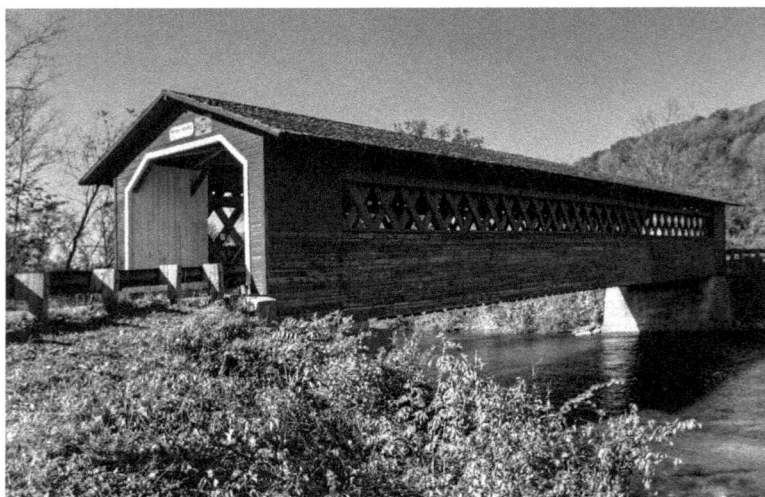

Township: Bennington
County: Bennington

GPS Position: N 42° 54.737' W 73° 15.288'
Directions: From the town of North Bennington, go south on Buckley Road, continuing on Water St., for about 1.3 miles. Turn left on River Road and the bridge is a short distance.

Crosses: Walloomsac River
Carries: River Road

Builder: Original not known. 1989 Blow and Cote
Year Built: 1989 (Rebuild of original 1840)
Truss Type: Town
Dimensions: 1 Span, 121 Feet

Photo Tip: A nice quiet setting with easy views from all sides.

Notes: None of the original materials was used in the rebuild. The original had its Town trusses doubled to increase its load capacity but the current bridge is a single Town truss.

World Index Number: 45-02-02#2
National Register of Historic Places: August 28, 1973

Paper Mill Covered Bridge

Township: Bennington
County: Bennington

GPS Position: N 42° 54.776' W 73° 13.992'
Directions: In the town of North Bennington go south on Murphy Road off of VT-67A/ North Bennington Road and the bridge is a short distance.

Crosses: Walloomsac River
Carries: Murphy Road

Builder: Original Charles F. Sears (Rebuild by Blow and Cote)
Year Built: 2000 rebuild of the original 1889 bridge

Truss Type: Town
Dimensions: 1 Span, 126 Feet

Photo Tip: You need to watch for posted private property but there are good vantage points for the front and sides.
Notes: The original bridge was demolished in 1999 and its replacement was completed in 2000 as the cost of repairs exceeded the price of a new bridge. It is built in an authentic manner and the fresh barn red paint job looks excellent.

World Index Number: 45-02-03#2
National Register of Historic Places: Original bridge August 28, 1973

Silk Covered Bridge
(Locust Grove Covered Bridge)

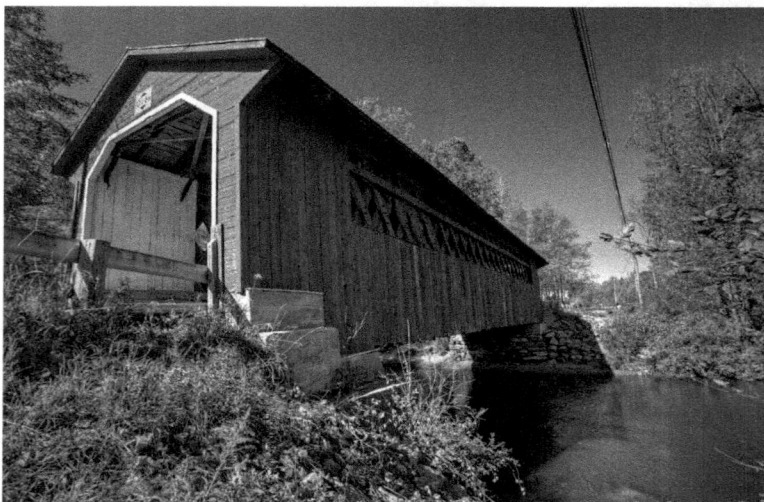

Township: Bennington
County: Bennington

GPS Position: N 42° 54.577' W 73° 13.519'

Directions: In the town of North Bennington go south on Silk Road off of VT-67A/ North Bennington Road and the bridge is a short distance.

Crosses: Walloomsac River
Carries: Silk Road

Builder: Benjamin Sears
Year Built: Ca1840 (R1952) (R1985) (R1991)
Truss Type: Town
Dimensions: 1 Span, 88 Feet

Photo Tip: Easy from all sides.
Notes: This is a lovely bridge in a natural setting. The barn red paint is nicely set off by white on the portal trim

World Index Number: 45-02-04
National Register of Historic Places: August 28, 1973

Chiselville Covered Bridge

Township: Sunderland

County: Bennington

GPS Position: N 43° 04.345' W 73° 07.959'
Directions: From the town of East Arlington take Maple St. and continue on Sunderland Hill Rd northeast and the bridge site is about 1 mile

Crosses: Batten Kill
Carries: Sunderland Hill Rd

Builder: Daniel Oatman
Year Built: 1870 (R1972) (R1996)
Truss Type: Town
Dimensions: 2 Span, 117 Feet, the center steel pier was added in 1973

Photo Tip: Front and 3/4 shots only. The river is 40 feet below down steep banks making side views difficult.
Notes: Named after a Chisel Factory which was formerly in the area. It replaced a bridge washed out in 1869.

World Index Number: 45-02-05
National Register of Historic Places: Not listed

Caledonia County

Greenbanks Hollow Covered Bridge

Township: Danville
County: Caledonia

GPS Position: N 44° 22.644' W 72° 07.328'
Directions: From the town of Danville take Brainerd St. south from US-2 and continue on Greenbanks Hollow Road. You will find the bridge after 2.7 miles. If approaching from east of Danville, be careful that your GPS doesn't lead you astray on small roads. You want to go from the town of Danville.

Crosses: Joe's Brook
Carries: Greenbanks Hollow Road

Builder: Not known
Year Built: 1886 (Substantially rebuilt in 2002)
Truss Type: Queenpost
Dimensions: 1 Span, 74 Feet

Photo Tip: Open from all sides

Notes: The 2002 rebuild made many changes to take out non-authentic elements. It is in a quiet spot and looks great with its partially open sides.

World Index Number: 45-03-01#2
National Register of Historic Places: June 13, 1974

Schoolhouse Covered Bridge

Township: Lyndon
County: Caledonia

GPS Position: N 44° 30.977' W 72° 00.591'
Directions: From the town of Lyndon go south on US-5 past I-91 and after 0.8 miles turn right on South Wheelock Rd. The parking lot for the bridge is a short distance.

Crosses: South Wheelock Branch of Passumpsic River
Carries: South Wheelock Rd. (Bypassed)

Builder: J.C. Jones, Lee Goodell and John Clement
Year Built: 1879 (R1959) (R1971)

Truss Type: Queenpost
Dimensions: 1 Span, 42 Feet

Photo Tip: Easy from all sides.
Notes: The trusses have been enclosed and painted while there is only one walkway instead of the original two. A very nice looking bridge in a park like setting.

World Index Number: 45-03-03
National Register of Historic Places: March 31, 1971

Chamberlin Covered Bridge
(Whitcomb Covered Bridge)

Township: Lyndon
County: Caledonia

GPS Position: N 44° 30.963' W 72° 00.876'
Directions: From I-91 take Exit 23, south of the town of Lyndon and go east on US-5 for 0.4 miles and then turn right onto Chamberlin Bridge Rd. The bridge is a short distance.

Crosses: Passumpsic River
Carries: Chamberlin Bridge Rd. Sometimes spelled Chamberlain Bridge Road
Builder: Not known
Year Built: 1881 (R2002)
Truss Type: Queen
Dimensions: 1 Span, 66 Feet

Photo Tip: Easy portal views although you need to watch for traffic. There are not easy side views.
Notes: The original bridge was an open one which was covered in 1881. At one point it seems to have been relegated to a walkway and wood storage but it currently carries vehicle traffic.

World Index Number: 45-03-04
National Register of Historic Places: July 30, 1974

Sanborn Covered Bridge
(Center Covered Bridge)

Township: Lyndon
County: Caledonia

GPS Position: N 44° 32.628' W 72° 00.055'
Directions: From the town of Lyndon go to the north end on US-5. The bridge site is just south of the intersection with Stevens Loop

Crosses: Passumpsic River
Carries: Private lane

Builder: Not known
Year Built: 1867 (M1960) (R2002)
Truss Type: Paddleford
Dimensions: 1 Span, 117 Feet

Photo Tip: Easy from all sides.
Notes: One of only three Vermont bridges using the Paddleford Truss. During a visit in 2011, this bridge was looking quite ragged. Privately owned, it was moved to this location in 1960.

World Index Number: 45-00-00
National Register of Historic Places: June 20, 1974

Miller's Run Covered Bridge
(Bradley Covered Bridge)

Township: Lyndon
County: Caledonia

GPS Position: N 44° 32.533' W 72° 00.596'
Directions: From the village of Lyndon Center go north on Center St. for 0.2 miles where you will see the site.

Crosses: Miller's Run
Carries: Center St.

Builder: E.H. Stone (Plans)
Year Built: 1995 Restoration of original bridge built in 1878
Truss Type: Queenpost
Dimensions: 1 Span, 56 Feet

Photo Tip: Good views from all sides but watch for traffic.
Notes: This bridge was restored using some of the timbers from the original 1878 bridge. It has a walkway for pedestrians and continues to serve vehicle traffic.

World Index Number: 45-03-06
National Register of Historic Places: June 13, 1977 (Original)

Old Burrington Covered Bridge
(Randall Covered Bridge)

Township: Lyndon
County: Caledonia

GPS Position: N 44° 33.198' W 71° 58.165'
Directions: From the town of Lyndon take US-5/ Main St. north and continue on VT-114/ Burke Rd for 1.7 miles and turn right onto Burrington Bridge Road. The bridge is a short distance.

Crosses: East Branch of the Passumpsic River
Carries: Burrington Bridge Road

Builder: Not known
Year Built: 1865

Truss Type: Queen
Dimensions: 1 Span, 68 Feet

Photo Tip: Easy from all sides
Notes: The bridge has been bypassed and in 2011 was not in the best condition

World Index Number: 45-03-07
National Register of Historic Places: June 13, 1974

Chittenden County

Holmes Covered Bridge
(Lake Shore Covered Bridge)

Township: Charlotte
County: Chittenden

GPS Position: N 44° 19.970' W 73° 16.940'
Directions: From the town of Charlotte, take Ferry Road west and, after 0.6 miles, turn right on Lake Road. The bridge site is then 1.8 miles.

Crosses: Holmes Creek
Carries: Lake Road

Builder: Not known
Year Built: 1870
Truss Type: King with Tied Arch
Dimensions: 1 Span, 41 Feet

Photo Tip: Easy views from all sides.

Notes: Found on the shore of Lake Champlain, it provides a beautiful setting. There is a municipal swimming area nearby, ideal for a family outing and picnic.

World Index Number: 45-45-04-01
National Register of Historic Places: September 6, 1974

Sequin Covered Bridge
(Upper, Brown's Covered Bridge)

Township: Charlotte
County: Chittenden

GPS Position: N 44° 17.333' W 73° 09.002'
Directions: From the Village of Monkton Ridge go north on Monkton Road and take a slight right onto Silver St. After 0.4 miles turn left on Rotax Road and continue for 1.9 miles where you turn right on Roscoe Road. The bridge site is about 1.8 miles.

Crosses: Lewis Creek
Carries: Roscoe Road

Builder: Not known
Year Built: 1850 (R1949) (R1978) (R1994) (R2002)
Truss Type: Multiple King with Burr Arch
Dimensions: 1 Span, 71 Feet

Photo Tip: All sides are available.
Notes: Very similar in construction to nearby Quinlin Covered Bridge and may well have had the same builder. In a nice quiet setting.

World Index Number: 45-04-02
National Register of Historic Places: September 6, 1974

Quinlin Covered Bridge
(Lower Covered Bridge)

Township: Charlotte
County: Chittenden

GPS Position: N 44° 16.559' W 73° 11.047'
Directions: From the town of Charlotte go east on Ferry road and turn right on US-7/ Ethan Allen Highway. After 2.5 miles turn left onto State Park Road and after a further 0.6 miles turn right onto Mt

Philo Road. After 0.9 miles make a sharp right on Spear St and continue 2.1 miles to the bridge site

Crosses: Lewis Creek
Carries: Spear St

Builder: Not known
Year Built: 1849 (R1950) (R1994)
Truss Type: Multiple King with Burr Arch
Dimensions: 1 Span 86 Feet

Photo Tip: Easy from all sides.
Notes: On a quiet road although the Creek can flood at times. Steel beams were installed under the floor at one time.

World Index Number: 45-04-03
National Register of Historic Places: September 10, 1974

Westford Covered Bridge
(Brown's River Covered Bridge)

Township: Charlotte

County: Chittenden

GPS Position: N 44° 36.748' W 73° 00.462'
Directions: In the town of Westford go east off VT-128 on
Cambridge Road. The bridge site is a short distance.

Crosses: Brown's River
Carries: Cambridge Road

Builder: Not known
Year Built: 1837 (R1976) (R2001)
Truss Type: Multiple King with Burr Arch
Dimensions: 1 Span, 97 Feet

Photo Tip: Good 3/4 views available.
Notes: The bridge was closed to traffic in 1965 and it was feared it
would collapse. Through the years attempts to raise funds and save it
were made and it was finally return to a bypassed section in 2001 after
being rebuilt.

World Index Number: 45-04-05
National Register of Historic Places: Not listed

Cambridge Village Covered Bridge
(Museum, Shelburne Covered Bridge)

Township: Shelburne
County: Chittenden

GPS Position: N 44° 22.397' W 73° 13.859'
Directions: In the town of Shelburne, the bridge is located at the
Shelburne Museum just off US-7/ Shelburne Rd between Harbor Rd
and Bostwick Rd.

Crosses: Burr Pond
Carries: Cambridge Road (Bypassed)

Builder: George William Holmes

Year Built: 1845 (M1951) (R1998)
Truss Type: Multiple King with Burr Arch
Dimensions: 1 Span, 163 Feet

Photo Tip: There is an admission charge although you can take pictures from the public street.
Notes: Originally located in Cambridge, Vermont, it was bypassed by a steel bridge, and was donated to the Shelburne Museum. It was dismantled and moved to its present location in 1951. It has two lanes which were used for vehicles plus a pedestrian walkway

World Index Number: 45-00-00
National Register of Historic Places: Not listed

Essex County

Columbia Covered Bridge

Nearest Town: Columbia, New Hampshire and Lemington, Vermont
County: Coos County, New Hampshire and Essex, Vermont

GPS Position: N 44° 51.159' W 71° 33.050'
Directions: Take Vermont-102 south from the Lemington area and turn left on Bridge St. The bridge is a short distance. From the New Hampshire side, take New Hampshire-26/ Us-3 south from Columbia and turn right on the Columbia Bridge Rd. and follow a short way to the end.

Crosses: Connecticut River
Carries: Columbia Bridge Rd.

Builder: Charles Babbitt
Year Built: 1912 (R1981)
Truss Type: Howe
Dimensions: 1 span, 146 feet

Photo Tip: There are good views from all sides, especially the north side in New Hampshire

Notes: This is one of three covered bridges which span the Connecticut River between New Hampshire and Vermont. It replaced a covered bridge which was destroyed by fire in 1911.There are full length sideboards on the downstream side and half length on the upstream. The theory is that during a flood, the force of the water will pass through the upstream openings and push off the boards on the downstream. The river is narrow at this most northern bridge between Vermont and New Hampshire.

World Index Number: 45-05-02 (Vermont) and 29-04-07 (New Hampshire)
National Register of Historic Places: December 12, 1976

Mount Orne Covered Bridge

Nearest Town: Lancaster, New Hampshire and Lunenburg, Vermont
County: Coos County, New Hampshire and Essex, Vermont

GPS Position: N 44° 27.634' W 71° 39.206'
Directions: From Lunenburg, Vermont take Us-2 east and turn right on River Road. After 0.3 miles, you will see the bridge entrance on the left. From Lancaster, New Hampshire go south on NH-135/ Elm St.

and you will reach the bridge entrance in a bit more than 5 miles. You will not be able to walk or drive through the bridge as it is closed.

Crosses: Connecticut River
Carries: Mount Orne Road (Closed)

Builder: Berlin Iron Bridge Co.
Year Built: 1911 (R1969) (R1983)
Truss Type: Howe
Dimensions: 2 spans, 266 feet

Photo Tip: There are good views from the north side bank on both sides of the river
Notes: This bridge replaced an open toll bridge built in the late 1800s. It was closed in 1983. It is said to produce a moaning sound in the right wind from the iron rods of its Howe truss. The bridge was re-opened in 2012

World Index Number: 45-05-03#2 (Vermont) and 29-04-03#2 (New Hampshire)
National Register of Historic Places: December 12, 1976

Franklin County

Hopkins Covered Bridge

Township: Enosburg
County: Franklin

GPS Position: N 44° 55.229' W 72° 40.366'
Directions: From the town of East Berkshire take State Route 118/ Montgomery Rd. east for 2.2 miles and then take a right onto Hopkins Bridge Road where you will see the bridge.

Crosses: Trout River
Carries: Hopkins Bridge Road

Builder: Sheldon & Savannard Jewett
Year Built: 1875 (Rebuilt 1999)
Truss Type: Town
Dimensions: 1 Span, 90 Feet

Photo Tip: Easy views from all sides.
Notes: Extensive repairs were made in 1999 and the bridge looks in excellent condition.

World Index Number: 45-06-01#2
National Register of Historic Places: November 30, 1974

Maple Street Covered Bridge
(Village, Lower Covered Bridge)

Township: Fairfax
County: Franklin

GPS Position: N 44° 39.803' W 73° 00.630'
Directions: In the town of Fairfax take Maple St south off VT-104/ Main St. and the bridge is about 0.2 miles.

Crosses: Mill Brook
Carries: Maple St

Builder: Kingsbury and Stone
Year Built: 1865 (R1975) (R1991) (R1998) (R2002)
Truss Type: Town
Dimensions: 1 Span, 57 Feet

Photo Tip: Although right in the town of Fairfax, it is in a natural setting, easy views from front and sides.

Notes: The 1927 flood which destroyed many covered bridges, washed this one downstream and when it was returned it was said to have been restored with the west end facing east, and has caused a slight permanent lean.

World Index Number: 45-06-02
National Register of Historic Places: November 4, 1974

East Fairfield Covered Bridge

Township: Fairfield
County: Franklin

GPS Position: N 44° 47.168' W 72° 51.719'
Directions: In the town of East Fairfield, look for Bridge St. just off VT-36. The bridge site is only a short distance.

Crosses: Black Creek
Carries: Bridge St.

Builder: Not known
Year Built: 1865 (R1940s) (R1967) (R1974) (R2009)
Truss Type: Queen
Dimensions: 1 Span, 67 Feet

Photo Tip: There are good views from all sides. Black Creek provides good reflections in side views.
Notes: Since the completion of the 2009 repairs, this bridge is again open for vehicle traffic and looks in excellent condition.

World Index Number: 45-06-03
National Register of Historic Places: November 19, 1974

Comstock Covered Bridge

Township: Montgomery
County: Franklin

GPS Position: N 44° 53.969' W 72° 38.669'
Directions: From the town of Montgomery, go west on State Route 118 for 2.3 miles and turn left onto Comstock Bridge Rd. The bridge site is a short distance.

Crosses: Trout River

Carries: Comstock Bridge Rd.

Builder: Sheldon and Savannard Jewett
Year Built: 1883 (R1998) (R2004)
Truss Type: Town
Dimensions: 1 Span, 69 feet

Photo Tip: There are easy views all around but look for a longer shot from the side with the river in the foreground.
Notes: This is a very nice looking structure with unpainted sides and white portals and interior weather panels.

World Index Number: 45-06-04
National Register of Historic Places: November 19, 1974

Fuller Covered Bridge
(Blackfalls, Post Office Covered Bridge)

Township: Montgomery
County: Franklin

GPS Position: N 44° 54.199' W 72° 38.376'

Directions: From the town of Montgomery, take Main St./ State Route 118 northwest for 2.3 miles and turn right onto South Richford Road. The bridge is about 0.2 miles, near the intersection of Brook Rd.

Crosses: Black Falls Brook
Carries: South Richford Road

Builder: Sheldon and Savannah Jewett
Year Built: 1890 (R1981) (R1982) (R1997) (R2002)
Truss Type: Town
Dimensions: 1 Span, 50 Feet

Photo Tip: There are easy views from the fronts and sides
Notes: This is a bridge which has seen a few disasters from floods, truck damage, and even a Powder Post Beatle infestation. It seems to be a survivor and it has had a recent extensive renovation which included the removal of a non-authentic steel I-beam.

World Index Number: 45-06-05#2
National Register of Historic Places: December 23, 1974

Hectorville Covered Bridge In Storage
(Gibou Covered Bridge)

Township: Montgomery
County: Franklin

GPS Position: Was N 44° 51.196' W 72° 36.811'
Directions:

Crossed: South Branch of the Trout River
Carried:

Builder: Sheldon and Savannah Jewett
Year Built: 1883
Truss Type: Town and King
Dimensions: 1 Span, 54 Feet

Notes: Originally situated in Montgomery Village, it was moved to Hectorville in 1899. In 2002 the bridge was dismantled and placed in storage.

World Index Number: 45-06-06
National Register of Historic Places: Not listed

Hutchins Covered Bridge

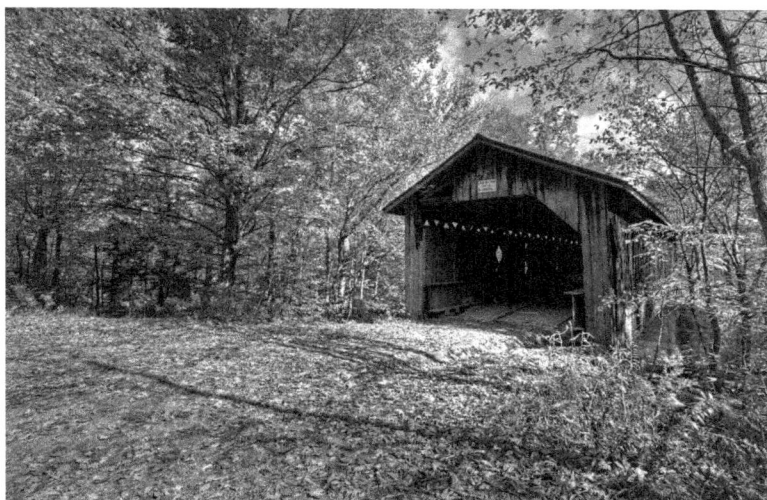

Township: Montgomery
County: Franklin

GPS Position: N 44° 51.520' W 72° 36.769'
Directions: from the town of Montgomery, go south on State Route 118/ Main St. for 1.2 miles and then turn right onto Hutchins Bridge Rd. The bridge site is a short distance.

Crosses: South Branch Trout River
Carries: Hutchins Bridge Rd.

Builder: Sheldon and Savannah Jewett
Year Built: 1883 (R1969) (R2002)

Truss Type: Town
Dimensions: 1 Span, 77 Feet

Photo Tip: This bridge is in a beautiful natural setting. There are large steel beams that make images a problem.
Notes: Sheldon and Savannah Jewett built all of the bridges that survive in the Montgomery area. This bridge has closed awaiting repair.

World Index Number: 45-06-07
National Register of Historic Places: December 30, 1974

Longley Covered Bridge
(Harnois, Head Covered Bridge)

Township: Montgomery
County: Franklin

GPS Position: N 44° 54.438' W 72° 39.333'
Directions: From the town of East Berkshire, take State Route 118/ Montgomery Rd southeast for 3.6 miles and turn right onto Longley Bridge Rd. The bridge is a short distance.

Crosses: Trout River
Carries: Longley Bridge Rd.

Builder: Sheldon and Savannah Jewett
Year Built: 1863 (R1979) (R1992)
Truss Type: Town
Dimensions: 1 Span, 85 Feet

Photo Tip: Easy views from all sides.
Notes: Found in a quiet country setting, the white portals look great against the weathered unpainted sides.

World Index Number: 45-06-08
National Register of Historic Places: December 30, 1974

West Hill Covered Bridge
(Creamery Covered Bridge)

Township: Montgomery
County: Franklin

GPS Position: N 44° 52.069' W 72° 38.868'
Directions: From the town of Montgomery go west on Main St/ State Route 118 for 2.6 miles and turn left onto Hill West Rd. After 2.4 miles turn right on Creamery Bridge Road and the bridge is a short distance.

If the roads are icy, you might be safer to park at the top and walk down as the roads either way from the bridge are steep.

Crosses: West Hill Brook
Carries: Creamery Bridge Road

Builder: Sheldon and Savannah Jewett
Year Built: 1883 (R2000) (R2009)
Truss Type: Town
Dimensions: 1 Span, 59 Feet

Photo Tip: There are side views with care and easy portal views.
Notes: This bridge had been closed to traffic in 1994 but the 2009 renovation has allowed it to re-open.

World Index Number: 45-06-09
National Register of Historic Places: December 31, 1974

Lamoille County

Grist Mill Covered Bridge
(Scott, Bryan, Canyon Covered Bridge)

Township: Cambridge
County: Lamoille

GPS Position: N 44° 38.195' W 72° 49.531'
Directions: From the town of Jeffersonville, take Mill St./ Vt-108 south for 0.7 miles and then left on Canyon Rd. The site is about 0.5 miles.

Crosses: Canyon Rd.
Carries: Brewster River

Builder: Not known
Year Built: 1872 (R1952) (R1970) (R2004)
Truss Type: Multiple Kingpost with Burr Arch
Dimensions: 1 Span, 85 feet

Photo Tip: There is an excellent side view from river level.
Notes: One of the bridges names is for a grist mill that used to be located nearby.

World Index Number: 45-08-01
National Register of Historic Places: June 13, 1974

Cambridge Junction Covered Bridge
(Poland or Station Covered Bridge)

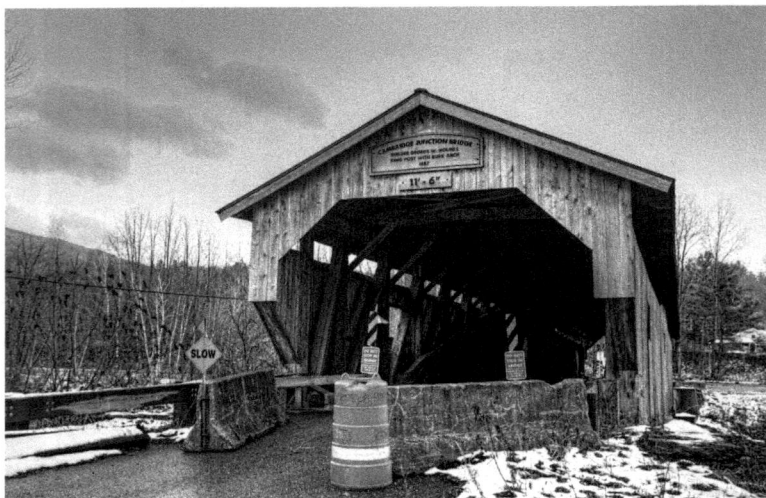

Township: Cambridge
County: Lamoille

GPS Position: N 44° 39.088' W 72° 48.798'
Directions: from the Town of Jeffersonville, take VT-108 north 0.4 miles and turn right on VT-109, and after 0.8 miles, another right onto Cambridge Junction Rd. to the bridge.

Crosses: Lamoille River
Carries: Cambridge Junction Rd.(Closed)

Builder: George H. Holmes
Year Built: 1887 (R2004)
Truss Type: Multiple Kingposts with Burr Arch
Dimensions: 1 Span, 153 feet

Photo Tip: Various barriers and traffic cones have made photography a bit of a problem at the moment. There are probably good side views available but the river was high when I was there.

Notes: The bridge and road are currently closed, and since there are nearby roads that can be used, it is problematic whether it may re-open. It is the second longest single span covered bridge in Vermont. It initially ran into problems in being built until Luke P. Poland, the former chief justice of the Vermont Supreme Court, made it his retirement project.

World Index Number: 45-08-02
National Register of Historic Places: October 9, 1974

Gates Farm Covered Bridge
(Little Covered Bridge)

Township: Cambridge
County: Lamoille

GPS Position: N 44° 38.741' W 72° 52.339'

Directions: From the town of Cambridge, take VT-15 northeast for about 0.3 miles and you will see the bridge on your right down a farm access road.

Crosses: Seymour River
Carries: Farm road

Builder: George W. Holmes
Year Built: 1897 (M1950) (R1995)
Truss Type: Multiple King with Burr Arch
Dimensions: 1 Span, 82 Feet

Photo Tip: You can take photographs from the public road, but note that closer views take you onto private land.
Notes: In 1950, the Seymour River course was changed and this bridge became unnecessary. The river course change separated the Gates farm from its fields and the bridge was moved to provide access to farm machinery.

World Index Number: 45-08-04#2
National Register of Historic Places: November 19, 1974

Lumber Mill Covered Bridge
(Lower Covered Bridge)

Township: Belvidere
County: Lamoille

GPS Position: N 44° 44.636' W 72° 44.476'
Directions: From Belvidere Junction take Back Road north off VT-109 and you will find the bridge in about 0.5 miles.

Crosses: North Branch of the Lamoille River
Carries: Back Road

Builder: Lewis Robinson
Year Built: 1895 (R1972) (R1995) (R2001)
Truss Type: Queen
Dimensions: 1 Span, 71 Feet

Photo Tip: Good views from all sides particularly a side view from the river bank.
Notes: After a 1971 truck accident, steel beams and concrete abutments were added. It is located in a pleasant setting.

World Index Number: 45-08-06
National Register of Historic Places: November 19, 1974

Morgan Covered Bridge
(Upper Covered Bridge)

Township: Belvidere
County: Lamoille

GPS Position: N 44° 44.616' W 72° 43.684'
Directions: From Belvidere Junction go east on VT-109 for 0.8 miles and turn left on Morgan Bridge Road. The bridge is a short distance.

Crosses: North Branch of the Lamoille River
Carries: Morgan Bridge Road

Builder: Lewis Robinson
Year Built: 1887 (R1898) (R2001)

Truss Type: Queen
Dimensions: 1 Span, 65 Feet

Photo Tip: Easy from all sides and from river level.
Notes: Unlike nearby bridges, this one has not had steel beams added. Found in a quiet natural setting.

World Index Number: 45-08-07
National Register of Historic Places: November 19, 1974

Power House Covered Bridge
(School Street Covered Bridge)

Township: Johnson
County: Lamoille

GPS Position: N 44° 38.161' W 72° 40.198'
Directions: From the town of Johnson take VT-100C northeast off VT-15/ Lower Main St. and the bridge is about 0.4 miles just left at School House Street.

Crosses: Gihon River

Carries: School House Street

Builder: Not known
Year Built: 2002 Rebuild of the 1872 original
Truss Type: Queen and King
Dimensions: 1 Span, 63 Feet

Photo Tip: Good views from all sides.
Notes: The 2002 reconstruction was required because the original 1872 bridge collapsed under the weight of snow. The steel beams added in about 1995 were retained in the rebuilt building.

World Index Number: 45-08-08#2
National Register of Historic Places: October 9, 1974

Scribner Covered Bridge
(DeGoosh, Mudget Covered Bridge)

Township: Johnson
County: Lamoille

GPS Position: N 44° 38.383' W 72° 38.911'

Directions: From the town of East Johnson go east on VT-100C for 0.5 miles and turn right on Rocky Road. The bridge is found in about 0.3 miles.

Crosses: Gihon River
Carries: Rocky Road

Builder: Not known
Year Built: Ca1919
Truss Type: Modified Queen
Dimensions: 1 Span, 48 Feet

Photo Tip: Easy from all sides.
Notes: The bridge was uncovered until about 1919 when it was renovated as a covered bridge. At some point steel beams were added as well as cement abutments. It is a quiet setting.

World Index Number: 45-08-09
National Register of Historic Places: October 1, 1974

Red Covered Bridge
(Sterling Brook, Chaffee Covered Bridge)

Township: Morriston
County: Lamoille

GPS Position: N 44° 31.109' W 72° 40.669'
Directions: From Morriston go east on Walton Road and turn left onto Cole Road after 0.7 miles. The bridge is about 3.9 miles

Crosses: Sterling Brook
Carries: Cole Road

Builder: Not known
Year Built: 1896 (R1971) (R2002)
Truss Type: King and Queen with iron rods
Dimensions: 1 Span, 64 Feet

Photo Tip: Easy from all sides.

Notes: Shortly after it was built it was twisted in a windstorm and iron rods were added to the truss system to strengthen it. A great looking bridge in a natural setting.

World Index Number: 45-08-11
National Register of Historic Places: October 16, 1974

Emily's Covered Bridge
(Stowe Hollow, Gold Brook Covered Bridge)

Township: Stowe
County: Lamoille

GPS Position: N 44° 26.422' W 72° 40.788'
Directions: From the town of Stowe go southeast on VT-108 for 1.1 miles and turn left on VT-100 and then the third right on School St. School St. becomes Stowe Hollow Rd., and then Covered Bridge Rd. and you will find the bridge site after about 2 miles.

Crosses: Gold Brook
Carries: Covered Bridge Rd.

Builder: John W. Smith
Year Built: 1844
Truss Type: Howe

Dimensions: 1 Span, 49 Feet

Photo Tip: There are nice tree shaded portal views as well as access to one side.
Notes: The older name of Stowe Hollow Covered Bridge has been supplanted by Emily's Bridge and various tales of her haunting the bridge. There are different stories about Emily but they all end in her tragic death at the bridge, so I guess her haunting is justified.

World Index Number: 45-08-12
National Register of Historic Places: October 1, 1974

Village Covered Bridge
(Church Street Covered Bridge)

Township: Waterville
County: Lamoille

GPS Position: N 44° 41.399' W 72° 46.262'
Directions: In the town of Waterville go east off VT-109 on Church Street and the bridge is a short distance.

Crosses: North Branch of the Lamoille River
Carries: Church Street

Builder: Not known
Year Built: Ca1877 (R1968) (R2000)
Truss Type: Queen
Dimensions: 1 Span, 61 Feet

Photo Tip: Easy from all sides
Notes: The bridge was reinforced with steel beams in 1968 after a truck damaged it the previous year. Further truck damage caused its closing in 1999.

World Index Number: 45-08-13
National Register of Historic Places: December 16, 1974

Montgomery Covered Bridge
(Lower, Potter Covered Bridge)

Township: Waterville
County: Lamoille

GPS Position: N 44° 42.348' W 72° 45.616'
Directions: From Belvidere Junction go south on VT-109 for 2.3 miles and turn left onto Montgomery Road where you will see the bridge.

Crosses: North Branch of the Lamoille River
Carries: Montgomery Road

Builder: Not known
Year Built: 1887 (R1969) (R1971) (R1997)
Truss Type: Queen
Dimensions: 1 Span, 70 Feet

Photo Tip: Easy from all sides and especially interesting from the rocks at the river.
Notes: After problems with the snow load and then damage by a loaded truck, steel beams were added in 1971 to increase the load capacity.

World Index Number: 45-08-14
National Register of Historic Places: October 18, 1974

Jaynes Covered Bridge
(Codding Hollow, Upper Covered Bridge)

Township: Waterville
County: Lamoille

GPS Position: N 44° 42.719' W 72° 45.388'
Directions: From the town of Belvidere Junction go south on VT-109 for 1.8 miles and turn left on Codding Hollow Rd. The bridge is a short distance.

Crosses: North Branch of the Lamoille River
Carries: Codding Hollow Rd.

Builder: Not known
Year Built: c1877 (R1960) (R2001)
Truss Type: Queenpost
Dimensions: 1 Span, 56 Feet

Photo Tip: Not an easy bridge to get a sideview due to brush and shrubs.
Notes: This bridge has had steel beams reinforcing it after a 1960 accident when a gravel filled truck fell through the floor.

World Index Number: 45-08-06
National Register of Historic Places: October 1, 1974

Fisher Railroad Covered Bridge
(Chubb, Chub Covered Bridge)

Township: Wolcot
County: Lamoille

GPS Position: N 44° 31.936' W 72° 25.660'
Directions: from the village of Potterville go east on VT-15 for 1.6 mile and you will see the bridge in a roadside park.

Crosses: Lamoille River
Carries: Railroad Line (Abandoned)

Builder: St. Johnsbury and Lamoille County Railroad

Year Built: 1908
Truss Type: Town-Pratt
Dimensions: 1 Span, 98 Feet

Photo Tip: There are terrific shots available from the portal and sides and the truss system is interesting as well.
Notes: This is one of just 2 covered railroad bridges surviving in Vermont. It is a wonderful structure with an interesting cupola on the top which was used to vent smoke from the railway engine. The rail line is gone except a set of tracks through the building, which adds to the character.

World Index Number: 45-08-16
National Register of Historic Places: October 1, 1974

Orange County

Moxley Covered Bridge
(Guy Covered Bridge)

Township: Chelsea
County: Orange

GPS Position: N 43° 57.436' W 72° 27.816'
Directions: From the town of North Turnbridge go north on VT-110 for 3.4 miles and turn right onto Moxley Rd. The bridge is a short distance.

Crosses: First Branch of the White River
Carries: Moxley Rd

Builder: Arthur C. Adams
Year Built: 1883 (R2001)
Truss Type: Queen and King
Dimensions: 1 Span, 56 Feet

Photo Tip: Open on all sides

Notes: On a quiet road with hills in the background, it makes a pleasant stop. Its shape is actually not square as it is built to conform to the road which is angled to the river.

World Index Number: 45-09-01
National Register of Historic Places: September 10, 1974

Gilford Covered Bridge
(C.K. Smith, Lower Covered Bridge)

Township: Randolph
County: Orange

GPS Position: N 43° 54.977' W 72° 33.330'
Directions: From the town of East Randolph go south on VT-14 for 1.6 miles and turn right onto Hyde Road where you will see the bridge

Crosses: South Branch of the White River
Carries: Hyde Road

Builder: Not known
Year Built: 1904 (R1985) (R2001)

Truss Type: Multiple King
Dimensions: 1 Span, 54 Feet

Photo Tip: Open from all sides
Notes: This bridge has a lower and upper level of kingpost trusses and it has been suggested that it was once uncovered. It currently has a fresh coat of orange-red paint and looks great

World Index Number: 45-09-03
National Register of Historic Places: July 30, 1974

Braley Covered Bridge
(Johnson, Upper, Blaisdell Covered Bridge)

Township: Randolph
County: Orange

GPS Position: N 43° 55.704' W 72° 33.337'
Directions: From the village of East Randolph go south on VT-14 for 0.7 miles and turn right on Braley Road. This road is sometimes called Blaisdell or Braley Covered Bridge Road and there doesn't seem to be a signpost for it. The bridge is about 0.3 miles.

Crosses: Second Branch of White River
Carries: Braley Road

Builder: Not known
Year Built: 1904 (R1090) (R1977) (R2004)
Truss Type: Multiple Kingpost
Dimensions: 1 Span, 38 Feet

Photo Tip: Good side and front views
Notes: Originally built in 1883 as an uncovered box pony with kingpost, it was given another half height layer of multiple kingposts when roofed in 1904. The only other bridge like this is nearby Guilford Covered Bridge. Be careful driving or walking in this area for other traffic

World Index Number: 45-09-04
National Register of Historic Places: June 13, 1974

Kingsbury Covered Bridge
(Hyde, South Randolph Covered Bridge)

Township: Randolph

County: Orange

GPS Position: N 43° 52.850' W 72° 34.903'
Directions: From the village of East Randolph go south on VT-14 for 4.3 miles and turn right onto Kingsbury Rd where you will find the bridge.

Crosses: Second Branch of the White River
Carries: Kingsbury Rd

Builder: Not known
Year Built: 1904 (R1958) (R1980) (R1994) (R2002)
Truss Type: Multiple Kingpost
Dimensions: 1 Span, 51 Feet

Photo Tip: Open on all sides
Notes: It looks in excellent condition, although vandalized by graffiti. It has no windows and is unpainted.

World Index Number: 45-09-02
National Register of Historic Places: July 30, 1974

Thetford Center Covered Bridge
(Sayres Covered Bridge)

Township: Thetford
County: orange

GPS Position: N 43° 49.939' W 72° 15.149'
Directions: From the village of Thetford Center go north on VT-113 for 0.3 miles and turn left on Tucker Hill Road. The bridge is found in a short distance.

Crosses: Ompompanoosuc River
Carries: Tucker Hill Road

Builder: Not known
Year Built: 1839 (R1963) (R1997)
Truss Type: Haupt (or Burr variation)
Dimensions: 1 span (with a later center pier added), 127 Feet

Photo Tip: Front and side setups are available.
Notes: In 1963 the center concrete pier was added to allow for heavier traffic load. The 1997 repairs were required after a truck attempted to drive through with its bed raised, destroying part of the ceiling supports.

World Index Number: 45-09-06
National Register of Historic Places: September 17, 1974

Union Village Covered Bridge

Township: Thetford
County: Orange

GPS Position: N 43° 47.321' W 72° 15.223'
Directions: From the village of Thetford Hill go south on Academy Rd off of VT-113 and the bridge is about 2.7 miles

Crosses: Ompompanoosuc River
Carries: Academy Rd

Builder: Not known

Year Built: (R1970) (R2002)
Truss Type: Multiple King Variation
Dimensions: 1 Span, 111 Feet

Photo Tip: Easy from all sides.
Notes: It is essential a multiple Kingpost truss system with the addition of two long diagonals which may act as an arch. The ceiling trusses are also massive and interesting. The three large windows provide a nice balanced look.

World Index Number: 45-09-05
National Register of Historic Places: September 17, 1974

Howe Covered Bridge

Township: Tunbridge
County: Orange

GPS Position: N 43° 51.890' W 72° 29.901'
Directions: From the village of Tunbridge go south on VT-110 for 3 miles and turn left on Belknap Brook Rd where you will see the bridge.

Crosses: First Branch of the White River
Carries: Belknap Brook Rd

Builder: Ira Mudget, Edward Wells and Chauncey Tenney
Year Built: 1879 (R1994) (R2002)
Truss Type: Multiple King
Dimensions: 1 Span, 75 Feet

Photo Tip: Views from all sides but a bit of shrubs on the side views.
Notes: The Kingpost also have vertical bars through the diagonal members. There is an old homemade ladder kept on one interior wall which apparently is there by long tradition rather than any current use.

World Index Number: 45-09-07
National Register of Historic Places: September 10, 1974

Hayward Covered Bridge
(Noble, Mill Covered Bridge)

Township: Tunbridge
County: Orange

GPS Position: N 43° 53.485' W 72° 29.486

Directions: In the town of Tunbridge, the bridge is just north on Spring Road.

Crosses: First Branch of White River
Carries: Spring Road

Builder: Original by Arthur C. Adams
Year Built: 2000 (Rebuild of original 1883 bridge)
Truss Type: Multiple King
Dimensions: 1 Span, 72 Feet

Photo Tip: There is a good side view fro the east side of spring road on the north end of the bridge but be careful of traffic.
Notes: The original structure was destroyed by an ice jam in 1999 and replaced by the current authentic structure the next year.

World Index Number: 45-09-09#2
National Register of Historic Places: July 30, 1974 (Original structure)

Cilley Covered Bridge
(Lower Covered Bridge)

Township: Tunbridge
County: Orange

GPS Position: N 43° 52.977' W 72° 30.256'
Directions: from the village of Tunbridge go south on VT-100 for about 1.5 miles and turn right onto Howe Lane. The bridge is about 0.2 miles.

Crosses: First Branch of the White River
Carries: Howe Lane

Builder: Arthur C. Adams
Year Built: 1883 (R2002)
Truss Type: Multiple Kingpost
Dimensions: 1 Span, 68 Feet

Photo Tip: Easy from all sides
Notes: Found in a quiet setting, it has low hills behind to set it off.

World Index Number: 45-09-08
National Register of Historic Places: September 10, 1974

Larkin Covered Bridge

Township: Tunbridge
County: Orange

GPS Position: N 43° 55.381' W 72° 27.894'
Directions: From the town of Tunbridge go north on VT-110 for 2 miles and turn right onto Larkin Road. The bridge is a short distance.

Crosses: First Branch of the White River
Carries: Larkin Road

Builder: Arthur C. Adams
Year Built: 1902 (R2002)
Truss Type: Multiple Kingpost
Dimensions: 1 Span, 68 Feet

Photo Tip: Easily seen from all sides.
Notes: It can be seen from the main Highway VT-110. It is in a quiet setting and makes a pleasant visit.

World Index Number: 45-09-19
National Register of Historic Places: July 30,1974

Flint Covered Bridge

Township: Tunbridge
County: Orange

GPS Position: N 43° 56.956' W 72° 27.495'
Directions: From the town of Tunbridge go north on VT-110 for 3.9 miles and turn right on Bicknell Hill Road. The bridge is a short distance.

Crosses: First Branch of the White River
Carries: Bicknell Hill Road

Builder: Not known
Year Built: 1874 (R1969) (R2002)
Truss Type: King and Queen
Dimensions: 1 Span, 87 Feet

Photo Tip: Easy from all sides.
Notes: The oldest of the Tunbridge area bridges, it is a peaceful place to stop for a visit.

World Index Number: 45-09-11
National Register of Historic Places: September 10, 1974

Orleans County

Lords Creek Covered Bridge

Township: Irasburg
County: Orleans

GPS Position: N 44° 48.993' W 72° 15.971'
Directions: From the town of Orleans, take VT-58 west for 2.7 miles and turn right onto Covered Bridge Road. The bridge is about 1.2 miles.

Crosses: Black River
Carries: Covered Bridge Road

Builder: Not known
Year Built: 1881 (M1958)
Truss Type: Paddleford
Dimensions: 1 Span, 50 Feet

Photo Tip: Easy to see and view
Notes: Moved in 1958 and now on private road as access to farm.

World Index Number: 45-10-01

National Register of Historic Places: Not listed

Orne Covered Bridge
(Coventry, Lower Covered Bridge)

Township: Irasburg
County: Orleans

GPS Position: N 44° 51.641' W 72° 16.444'
Directions: From Coventry go west on Main St. off US-5 and after0.5 miles, a slight right onto Covered Bridge Road. The bridge is about 0.5 miles along this road.

Crosses: Black River
Carries: Covered Bridge Road

Builder: Original bridge built by J.D. Colton
Year Built: 1999 rebuild of the original 1881 bridge
Truss Type: Paddleford
Dimensions: 1 Span, 87 Feet

Photo Tip: Easy from all sides.

Notes: The original bridge was arsoned in 1997 and replaced with this near replica authentic bridge in 1999. It is one of a small number of surviving bridges using the Paddleford Truss system

World Index Number: 45-10-02#2
National Register of Historic Places: November 20, 1974 (Original)

River Road Covered Bridge
(School, Upper Covered Bridge)

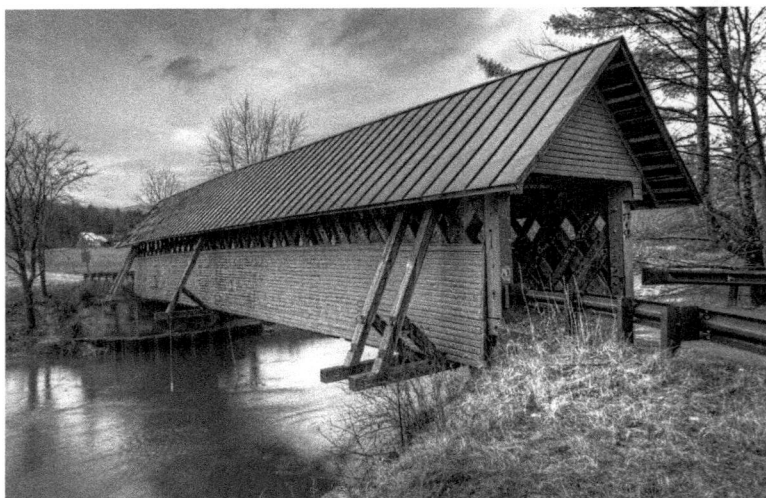

Township: Troy
County: Orleans

GPS Position: N 44° 57.377' W 72° 23.694'
Directions: From North Troy go south on VT-105/ Highland Ave for 2.1 miles and turn left on Veilleux Road to the intersection of River Road after 0.8 miles

Crosses: Missisquoi River
Carries: River Road

Builder: Not known

Year Built: 1910
Truss Type: Town
Dimensions: 1 Span, 93 Feet

Photo Tip: Easy views from all sides in a quiet natural setting.
Notes: A distinctive bridge with buttresses, partially exposed town truss and barn red color set off by a slate grey roof.

World Index Number: 45-10-03
National Register of Historic Places: November 19, 1974

Rutland County

Depot Covered Bridge

Township: Pittsford
County: Rutland

GPS Position: N 43° 42.577' W 73° 02.557'
Directions: From the town of Pittsford, go northwest on US-7 for 0.2 miles and turn right on Depot Hill Rd. The bridge is found in about 0.8 miles

Crosses: Otter Creek
Carries: Depot Hill Rd.

Builder: Not known
Year Built: 1840 (R1974) (R1985) (R2005)
Truss Type: Town
Dimensions: 1 Span, 121 Feet

Photo Tip: Good easy views from all sides.
Notes: It is quiet now but at one time it was near an active railroad station and from that it took its name. From the images, you can see that railway ties have been placed on a diagonal to stabilize the

structure from wind, something that the Town Truss has a weakness to.

World Index Number: 45-11-06
National Register of Historic Places: January 21, 1974

Sanderson Covered Bridge

Township: Brandon
County: Rutland

GPS Position: N 43° 47.367' W 73° 06.686'
Directions: From Brandon go south on Pearl Street off US-7. The bridge is 1.2 miles.

Crosses: Otter Creek
Carries: Pearl Street

Builder: Not known
Year Built: 2003 Rebuild of an 1840 Original
Truss Type: Town
Dimensions: 1 Span, 132 Feet

Photo Tip: Easy from all sides.
Notes: The original bridge was closed to vehicles and the rebuilt bridge was completed in 2003 allowing traffic to reopen. Some of the original bridge structure was used in the rebuild.

World Index Number: 45-11-02#2
National Register of Historic Places: Original June 13, 1974

Kingsley Covered Bridge
(Mill River Covered Bridge)

Township: Clarendon
County: Rutland

GPS Position: N 43° 31.418' W 72° 56.459'
Directions: From the Village of Cuttingsville take VT-103 northwest for 3.4 miles and turn left on Airport Rd, continuing on Gorge Rd/ River Rd. After 0.5 miles, turn left on East St. and the bridge is just ahead.

Crosses: Mill River
Carries: East St.

Builder: Timothy Horton
Year Built: 1836 (R1870) (R1950) (R1999) (R2002)
Truss Type: Town
Dimensions: 1 Span, 121 Feet

Photo Tip: There are good views near the mill if the water is not too high.
Notes: If the 1836 build date is correct, this is one of the oldest bridges in North America. Some claims say the 1870 repair was in fact a replacement. The restored Kingsley Mill is nearby.

World Index Number: 45-11-03
National Register of Historic Places: February 12, 1974

Cooley Covered Bridge

Township: Pittsford
County: Rutland

GPS Position: N 43° 41.427' W 73° 01.691'
Directions: From the town of Pittsford, go south off of Us-7 on Elm St. You will find the bridge site in a about 1 mile.

Crosses: Furnace Brook
Carries: Elm St.

Builder: Nichols Montgomery Powers
Year Built: 1849 (R2004)
Truss Type: Town
Dimensions: 1 Span, 51 feet

Photo Tip: This is a beautiful little bridge and looks terrific in its coat of barn red paint. Easy from all sides.
Notes: This bridge has been likened to a stranded Conestoga Wagon which it certainly resembles. The bridge is named after Benjamin Cooley, an early settler to the area and soldier in the Revolutionary War.

World Index Number: 45-11-07
National Register of Historic Places: January 24, 1974

Hammond Covered Bridge

Township: Pittsford

County: Rutland

GPS Position: N 43° 43.238' W 73° 03.239'
Directions: From the town of Pittsford, go northwest on US-7/ Franklin St. for 1 mile and turn left on Kendall Hill Road. The bridge site is about 0.8 miles.

Crosses: Otter Creek
Carries: Kendall Hill Road

Builder: Asa Nourse
Year Built: 1842 (R1927) (R2005)
Truss Type: Town
Dimensions: 1 Span, 139 Feet

Photo Tip: Easy views from all sides.
Notes: This is a great looking bridge in a quiet natural setting. Like many of the covered bridges at risk from the large flood of 1927, it suffered damage and was washed more than a mile downstream. It was floated back on empty barrels and replaced.

World Index Number: 45-11-05
National Register of Historic Places: January 21, 1974

Gorham Covered Bridge
(Goodnough Covered Bridge)

Township: Pittsford
County: Rutland

GPS Position: N 43° 40.798' W 73° 02.237'
Directions: Take VT-3/ Corn Hill Rd. south from Us-7 east of Pittsford for 2 miles and then make a right on Gorham Bridge Rd. The bridge is about 0.4 miles.

Crosses: Otter Creek
Carries: Gorham Bridge Rd

Builder: Abraham Owens & Nichols Powers
Year Built: 2004

Truss Type: Town
Dimensions: 1 Span, 115 Feet

Photo Tip: Excellent open looks from all sides.
Notes: This historically authentic bridge replaced the original built in 1842. Nichols Powers, one of the most famous of bridge builders, was Owen's apprentice but by the 1840s when the original was built, he had become his partner.

World Index Number: 45-11-04#2
National Register of Historic Places: February 12, 1974

Twin Covered Bridge

Township: Rutland
County: Rutland

GPS Position: N 43° 38.906' W 72° 58.319'
Directions: In the town of Rutland, it is located on the side of East Pittsford Road a mile north of US-7.

Crosses: On land

Carries: By Pittsford Road

Builder: Nichols Powers
Year Built: 1850
Truss Type: Town
Dimensions: 1 Span. 64 Feet

Photo Tip: Easy from all sides.
Notes: This bridge has had an interesting history but is currently in a sad state. It was one of two bridges built on side by side over East creek but was washed away in a flood in 1947 while its twin was destroyed. The flood was aggravated by a power company overextending a dam. The bridge was brought to its current position where it remains as a graffiti covered storage shed. The fact that it was constructed by a great historic builder, Nichols Powers, makes it's current fate even sadder.

World Index Number: 45-11-10
National Register of Historic Places: Not listed

Brown Covered Bridge
(Hollow Covered Bridge)

Township: Shrewsbury
County: Rutland

GPS Position: N 43° 33.962' W 72° 55.107'
Directions: From the town of North Clarendon, take Shrewsbury Rd. east off US-4 and continue on Cold River Rd. After 2.4 miles, go left on Upper Cold River Rd and the bridge is a short distance.

Crosses: Cold River
Carries: Upper Cold River Rd

Builder: Nichols Montgomery Powers
Year Built: 1880 (R2002)
Truss Type: Town
Dimensions: 1 Span, 112 feet

Photo Tip: It is in a hollow and you might want to plan on using a tripod, as it can be dark
Notes: This is the last bridge built by Nichols Powers when he was in his early sixties. It is said to be one of his finest structures.

World Index Number: 45-11-09
National Register of Historic Places: January 21, 1974

Washington County

A.M. Foster Covered Bridge

Township: Cabot
County: Washington

GPS Position: N 44° 25.416' W 72° 16.042'
Directions: from the village of Cabot, go northeast on Route 215 for 1.3 miles and turn right onto Cabot Plains Rd. After 1.6 miles, you will see the bridge in a field on your right.

Crosses: Pond
Carries: pedestrian

Builder: Richard Spaulding, Douglas Blondine, and Frank Foster
Year Built: 1988
Truss Type: Queenpost
Dimensions: 1 Span, 57 feet

Photo Tip: There are wide views from all sides with a millpond to offer reflections. It is on private property.

Notes: It was designed after the Martin Covered Bridge which still stands near Marshfield. It was named after the great-grandfather of one of the builders.

World Index Number: 45-12-75
National Register of Historic Places: Not listed

Coburn Covered Bridge
(Cemetery Covered Bridge)

Township: East Montpelier
County: Washington

GPS Position: N 44° 16.855' W 72° 27.233'
Directions: From the town of North Montpelier, go south on VT-14 for 0.8 miles and turn left on Coburn Road. After about 1 mile you will reach the bridge site.

Crosses: Winooski River
Carries: Coburn Road

Builder: Larned Coburn

Year Built: 1851 (R1961) (R1973) (R1997)
Truss Type: Queen and King
Dimensions: 1 Span, 69 feet

Photo Tip: Excellent portal plus side views from river level.
Notes: This bridge is currently unpainted which is apparently the original state of historic covered bridges. The builder, Larned Coburn, wanted the main road to be re-routed to go by his property and offered to build the bridge if it was. This offer was accepted.

World Index Number: 45-12-02
National Register of Historic Places: October 9, 1974

Martin Covered Bridge
(Orton Farm Covered Bridge)

Township: Marshfield
County: Washington

GPS Position: N 44° 17.255' W 72° 24.543'
Directions: from the town of North Montpelier go south on VT-214 for 1.9 miles and then turn left on US-2. The bridge is 1.6 miles.

Crosses: Winooski River
Carries: Farm road

Builder: Harry Martin
Year Built: 1890 (M2004) (R2009)
Truss Type: Queen
Dimensions: 1 Span, 45 Feet

Photo Tip: Easy from all sides
Notes: The bridge was moved to its present site after the town of Marshfield obtained it and the surrounding land in lieu of outstanding taxes. It is an excellent spot for a family outing and picnic.

World Index Number: 45-12-06
National Register of Historic Places: October 9, 1974

Chamberlin Covered Bridge
(Whitcomb Covered Bridge)

Township: Lyndon
County: Caledonia

GPS Position: N 44° 30.963' W 72° 00.876'
Directions: From I-91 take Exit 23, south of the town of Lyndon and go east on US-5 for 0.4 miles and then turn right onto Chamberlin Bridge Rd. The bridge is a short distance.

Crosses: Passumpsic River
Carries: Chamberlin Bridge Rd. Sometimes spelled Chamberlain Bridge Road

Builder: Not known
Year Built: 1881 (R2002)
Truss Type: Queen
Dimensions: 1 Span, 66 Feet

Photo Tip: Easy portal views although you need to watch for traffic. There are not easy side views.
Notes: The original bridge was an open one which was covered in 1881. At one point it seems to have been relegated to a walkway and wood storage but it currently carries vehicle traffic.

World Index Number: 45-03-04
National Register of Historic Places: July 30, 1974

Moseley Covered Bridge
(Stoney Creek Covered Bridge)

Township: Northfield
County: Washington

GPS Position: N 44° 07.709' W 72° 41.775'
Directions: from the town of Northfield take VT-12A south for 1.5 miles and turn right onto Stoney Brook Road. The bridge is about 1.5 miles.

Crosses: Stoney Brook
Carries: Stoney Brook Road

Builder: John Moseley
Year Built: 1899 (R1971) (R1978) (R1990)
Truss Type: King
Dimensions: 1 Span, 37 Feet

Photo Tip: Access to the sides is a bit obscured by brush.
Notes: Steel beams were added in 1971. The kingpost trusses are only part way up the sides but sufficient for a short span like this. It is unusual in being painted inside as well as out.

World Index Number: 45-12-07
National Register of Historic Places: November 20, 1974

Slaughter House Covered Bridge

Township: Northfield
County: Washington

GPS Position: N 44° 10.112' W 72° 39.268'
Directions: From the Town of Northfield Falls go east of VT-12 on Slaughter House Road. The bridge is a short distance.

Crosses: Dog River
Carries: Slaughter House Road

Builder: Not known
Year Built: 1872 (R1978() (R2002)

Truss Type: Queenpost
Dimensions: 1 Span, 60 Feet

Photo Tip: You can, with care, get to the river bank for side views.

Notes: Like the other area bridges, steel beams were added to strengthen it. The portals are rounded unlike other Vermont bridges.
World Index Number: 45-12-09
National Register of Historic Places: June 13, 1974

Second Covered Bridge
(Lower, Cox Brook, Newell Covered Bridge)

Township: Northfield
County: Washington

GPS Position: N 44° 10.366' W 72° 39.151'
Directions: In the town of Northfield Falls go east off of VT-12 on Cox Brook Road, to the second covered bridge. The first is the Station Covered Bridge.

Crosses: Cox Brook

Carries: Cox Brook Road

Builder: Not known
Year Built: 1872 (R1960) (R1978)
Truss Type: Queenpost
Dimensions: 1 Span, 57 Feet

Photo Tip: You can get this bridge and Station in the same image.
Notes: One of three covered bridges on this road with Station and Third Bridge. All are painted barn red.

World Index Number: 45-12-10
National Register of Historic Places: October 15, 1974

Station Covered Bridge
(Northfield Falls Covered Bridge)

Township: Northfield
County: Washington

GPS Position: N 44° 10.351' W 72° 39.084'

Directions: In the town of Northfield Falls the bridge is on Cox Brook Road just west of the intersection with VT-12

Crosses: Dog River
Carries: Cox Brook Road

Builder: Not known
Year Built: 1872 (R1963) (R1978) (R1993) (R2002)
Truss Type: Town
Dimensions: 2 Span (Center pier added in 1963), 137 Feet

Photo Tip: Side views are difficult and you need to be careful of traffic. You can get two bridges in the same image, this one and the Second Covered Bridge.
Notes: As well as having a pier added in 1963 it also had steel beams placed. It has two other bridges in the vicinity, Second and Third Covered Bridges, all three of which are painted red.

World Index Number: 45-12-08
National Register of Historic Places: August 13, 1974

Third Covered Bridge
(Upper Cox Brook Covered Bridge)

Township: Northfield
County: Washington

GPS Position: N 44° 10.425' W 72° 39.337'
Directions: In the town of Northfield Falls go east off of VT-12 on
Cox Brook Road, to the third covered bridge, about 0.3 miles. The first
two are the Station Covered Bridge and Second Covered Bridge.

Crosses: Cox Brook
Carries: Cox Brook Road

Builder: Not known
Year Built: Ca1872 (R1966) (R1978) (R2002)
Truss Type: Queenpost
Dimensions: 1 Span, 52 Feet

Photo Tip: You can with care get side views.
Notes: One of three covered bridges on this road with Station and
Second Bridge. All are painted barn red.

World Index Number: 45-12-11

National Register of Historic Places: October 1, 1974

Robbins Nest Covered Bridge

Township: Barre
County: Washington

GPS Position: N 44° 10.735' W 72° 28.261'
Directions: From the town of Barre take Washington St./ VT-302 southeast continuing on Eat Barre Road and after 1.3 miles, you will see the bridge on the right on a private road.

Crosses: Branch of Stevens Brook
Carries: Private Road

Builder: Robert R. Robbins
Year Built: 1964 (R1990) (R1993)
Truss Type: Queen
Dimensions: 1 Span, 57 Feet

Photo Tip: The bridge is on private property but it is easy to get images from the public roadside. Be careful as it has a lot of traffic.

Notes: The bridge is a private project which is a replica of a bridge washed away in a flood in 1927 which had been located nearby. Steel beams were added in 1990.

World Index Number: 45-12-18
National Register of Historic Places: Not listed

Pine Brook Covered Bridge
(Wilder Covered Bridge)

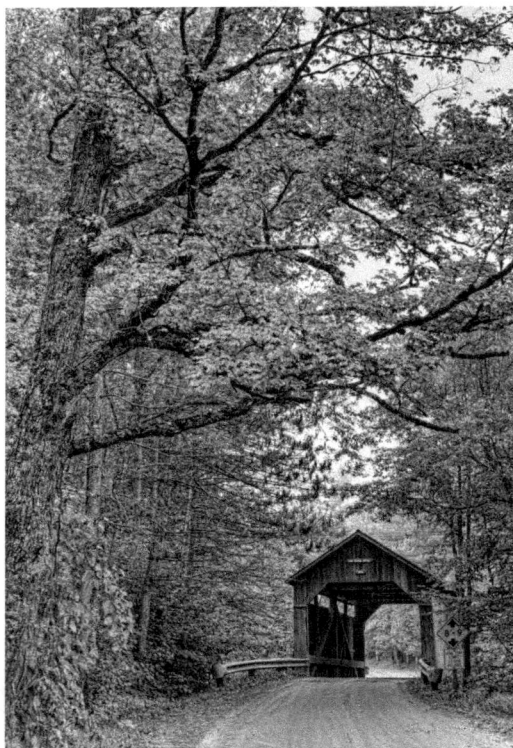

Township: Waitsfield
County: Washington

GPS Position: N 44° 12.339' W 72° 47.549'

Directions: From Waitsfield take VT-100 north for 1.4 miles and turn right onto Trembly Rd and then after 0.8 miles, left onto North Road. The bridge is then a short distance.

Crosses: Pine Brook
Carries: North Road

Builder: Not known
Year Built: 1872 (R1977) (R1989) (R2001)
Truss Type: Kingpost
Dimensions: 1 Span, 48 Feet

Photo Tip: Easy from all sides, and good long views.
Notes: In this quiet country setting, it would be easy to expect to see a horse and carriage to pass through this bridge. It was renovated by Milton Grafton in 1977.

World Index Number: 45-12-12
National Register of Historic Places: June 13, 1974

Big Eddy Covered Bridge
(Village, Great Eddy Covered Bridge)

Township: Waitsfield
County: Washington

GPS Position: N 44° 11.362' W 72° 49.409'
Directions: Found in the town of Waitsfield on Bridge St. just east of VT-100

Crosses: Mad River
Carries: Bridge St

Builder: Not known
Year Built: 1833
Truss Type: Multiple Kingpost with Burr Arch
Dimensions: 1 Span, 105 Feet

Photo Tip: The portal views can have a lot of traffic, good side views from the river bank.
Notes: Vermont's second oldest bridge, the walkway was added about 1940

World Index Number: 45-12-14
National Register of Historic Places: September 6, 1974

Warren Covered Bridge

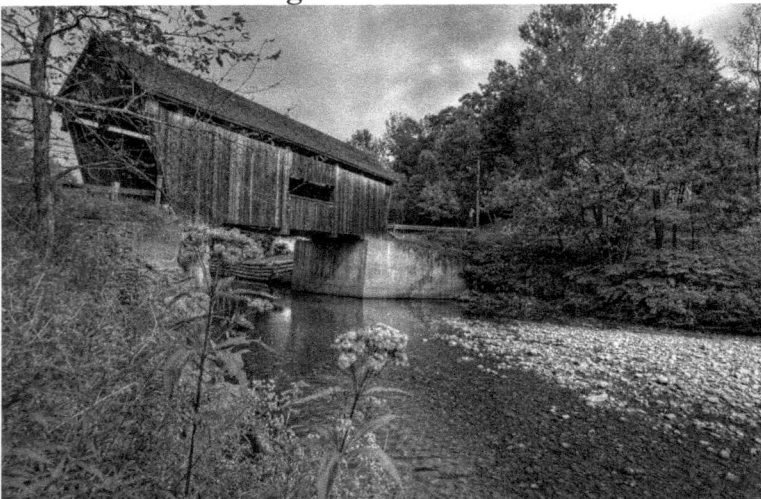

Township: Warren
County: Washington

GPS Position: N 44° 06.672' W 72° 51.411'
Directions: Found in the town of Warren on the Warren Bridge Road just east of Town Highway 44.

Crosses: Mad River
Carries: Warren Bridge Road

Builder: Walter Bagley
Year Built: 1880 (R1995) (R2000)
Truss Type: Queen
Dimensions: 1 Span, 55 Feet

Photo Tip: Easy from all sides.
Notes: The bridge was closed in 1998 for a major restoration and re-opened to traffic in 2000. It has interesting portals, one is built vertically while the other is on an angle.

World Index Number: 45-12-15
National Register of Historic Places: August 7, 1974

Windham County

Creamery Covered Bridge
(Centerville Covered Bridge)

Township: Brattleboro
County: Windham

GPS Position: N 42° 51.012' W 72° 35.119'
Directions: From I-91 north of Guilford, take Exit 2 onto VT-9 going west. After 0.3 miles turn left on Guildford St. and you will see the bridge.

Crosses: Whetstone River
Carries: Guildford St.

Builder: A crew of local workers
Year Built: 1879 (R1917)
Truss Type: Town
Dimensions: 1 Span, 80 Feet

Photo Tip: In the fall, there is a nice sideview with colorful sumac in the foreground. be careful of traffic, it can be busy.

Notes: This is the only bridge known to have a slate roof which was added in 1917. At one time it was highly decorated at Christmas including Santa and reindeer on the roof. it replaced a bridge washed away in a 1878 flood.

World Index Number: 45-13-01
National Register of Historic Places: August 28, 1973

West Dummerston Covered Bridge

Township: Dummerston
County: Windham

GPS Position: N 42° 56.170' W 72° 36.777'
Directions: From the town of Brattleboro go north on VT-30 for 5.78 miles and turn right on West Dummerston Covered Bridge Road where you will see the bridge.

Crosses: West River
Carries: West Dummerston Covered Bridge Road

Builder: Caleb Lamson

Year Built: 1998 Rebuild of an 1872 bridge (R1995)
Truss Type: Town
Dimensions: 2 Spans, 280 Feet

Photo Tip: There are great views from all sides. Look especially for a long sideview from the south. There is a convenient spot to pull off and set up.
Notes: This is one of the finest bridges in Vermont and it is in a great setting, particularly beautiful in the fall.

World Index Number: 45-13-02#2
National Register of Historic Places: May 8, 1973

Kidder Hill Covered Bridge

Township: Grafton
County: Windham

GPS Position: N 43° 10.119' W 72° 36.333'
Directions: From the town of Grafton, go south off VT-121/ Main St. on Kidder Hill Rd. and the bridge is 0.2 miles.

Crosses: South Branch of Saxton's River
Carries: Kidder Hill Rd.

Builder: Not known
Year Built: 1870 (R1950) (R1995)
Truss Type: Kingpost
Dimensions: 1 Span, 67 Feet

Photo Tip: There are great sideview from the river level which is easy to get to.
Notes: This bridge replaced a bridge destroyed in an 1869 flood. It is the longest of Vermont's Kingpost trussed bridges

World Index Number: 45-13-03
National Register of Historic Places: July 2, 1973

Green River Covered Bridge
(Village Covered Bridge)

Township: Guilford
County: Windham

GPS Position: N 42° 46.531' W 72° 40.018'
Directions: From I-91 just north of Guilford, take Exit 1 south on US-5 and go 1.4 miles where you turn right on Guilford Center Rd. After 4.6 miles turn right on Jacksonville Stage Rd and the bridge site is about 2.4 miles.

Crosses: Green River
Carries: Jacksonville Stage Rd

Builder: Marcus Worden
Year Built: 1870
Truss Type: Town
Dimensions: 1 Span, 104 Feet

Photo Tip: This is a great looking bridge and you will have no problem finding good views from all sides.
Notes: Just downstream from a dam, the Green River Covered bridge is an elegant structure with barn red portals set against its unpainted weathered sides. Up until 2001, the bridge housed local mailboxes.

World Index Number: 45-13-04
National Register of Historic Places: August 28, 1973

Williamsville Covered Bridge

Township: Newfane
County: Windham

GPS Position: N 42° 56.653' W 72° 44.306'
Directions: From the town of East Dover go east on Dover Hill Road for 2.4 miles where you will find the bridge.

Crosses: Rock River
Carries: Dover Hill Road

Builder: Eugene F. Wheller
Year Built: 1869 (R1950) (R1980) (R1990)
Truss Type: Town
Dimensions: 1 Span, 118 Feet

Photo Tip: There are views from all sides
Notes: Found in a natural setting and a spectacular one during the height of fall foliage.

World Index Number: 45-13-05
National Register of Historic Places: August 14, 1973

Hall Covered Bridge
(Park, Osgood Covered Bridge)

Township: Rockingham
County: Windham

GPS Position: N 43° 08.210' W 72° 29.267'
Directions: From the village of Saxtons River, go east on VT-121 for 1 mile and turn left on Hall Bridge Rd. where you will see the bridge.

Crosses: Saxton's River
Carries: Hall Bridge Rd.

Builder: Eugene P. Wheeler

Year Built: 1982 (Rebuild of original 1870 bridge)
Truss Type: Town
Dimensions: 1 Span, 121 Feet

Photo Tip: There are excellent side views which include the diamond shaped windows.
Notes: An overloaded truck damaged the original bridge in 1980, and the replacement was completed in 1982 by Milton Grafton who used a team of oxen to haul the bridge into place.

World Index Number: 45-13-07#2
National Register of Historic Places: August 28, 1973

Bartonsville Covered Bridge
(Williams River or Williams)

Township: Rockingham
County: Windham

GPS Position: N 43° 13.445' W 72° 32.230'

Directions: from the town of Rockingham, take VT-103/ Rockingham Rd east for 4.5 miles and turn right onto Lower Bartonsville Rd. The bridge is about 0.3 miles on the right.

Crosses: Williams River
Carries: Lower Bartonsville Rd.

Builder: Sanford Granger (Original)
Year Built: 1870 (R1983) (R2013)
Truss Type: Town
Dimensions: 1 Span, 151 feet

Photo Tips: Easy from all sides, especially a nice 3/4 view.
Notes: The bridge was swept away and destroyed from flood waters from Hurricane Irene. It was rebuilt in 2012 and re-opened in 2013.

World Index Number: 45-13-11#2
National Register of Historic Places: July 2, 1973

Victorian Village Covered Bridge
(Depot Covered Bridge)

Township: Rockingham
County: Windham

GPS Position: N 43° 11.680' W 72° 30.079'
Directions: From the town of Rockingham go northwest on VT-103 for 0.8 miles until you see the Vermont Country Store on the left. The bridge is on their property.

Crosses: Rock Brook
Carries: Pedestrian walkway

Builder: Sanford Grangers
Year Built: Originally 1872 Dismantled in 1959 and rebuilt in 1967 at current location
Truss Type: King
Dimensions: 1 Span, 44 Feet

Photo Tip: Easy from all sides. Note the nearby gristmill as well.
Notes: The bridge was originally built in Townshend, Vermont and was dismantled in 1959 by the Army Corps of Engineers when the

area was to be flooded. It was rebuilt as a shorter bridge with Kingpost trusses in 1967 at its current location.

World Index Number: 45-13-23
National Register of Historic Places: Not listed

Worrall Covered Bridge

Township: Rockingham
County: Windham

GPS Position: N 43° 12.702' W 72° 32.127'
Directions: From Rockingham take VT-103 northeast for 3.4 miles and turn right onto Williams Road. The bridge is a short distance.

Crosses: William's River
Carries: Williams Road

Builder: Sanford Granger
Year Built: 1868 (R1936) (R1970) (R2009) (R2012)
Truss Type: Town
Dimensions: 1 Span, 83 Feet

Photo Tip: Easy from all sides.

Notes: In the fall of 2009, this bridge was under repairs. It also suffered from flood damage from Hurricane Irene in August of 2011. By 2012, it had re-opened and looks excellent.

World Index Number: 45-13-10
National Register of Historic Places: July 16, 1973

Scott Covered Bridge

Township: Townshend
County: Windham

GPS Position: N 43° 02.930' W 72° 41.789'

Directions: From the town of Townshend go east of VT-30 for 1.5 miles and the bridge will be on your left.

Crosses: West River
Carries: Scott Bridge Road (Bypassed)

Builder: Harrison Chamberlin
Year Built: 1870
Truss Type: Town and King with Burr Arch
Dimensions: 3 Spans, 276 Feet

Photo Tip: One of Vermont's great bridges, it can be viewed from all sides as well as good long side views.
Notes: Although built in 1870, it wasn't covered until 1873. A concrete pier was added in 1981. The different spans were built as separate units , so the structure is actually three bridges joined. The Town truss section is the longest span in Vermont at 166 feet. It was closed to traffic in 1955.

World Index Number: 45-13-13
National Register of Historic Places: August 28, 1973

Windsor County

Best's Covered Bridge
(Swallows Covered Bridge)

Township: West Windsor
County: Windsor

GPS Position: N 43° 27.300' W 72° 30.986'
Directions: From the town of Fletchville, take VT-106 north for 1 mile and turn right onto VT-44. After 1.5 miles turn right onto Churchill Road and the bridge is just ahead of you.

Crosses: Mill Brook
Carries: Churchill Road

Builder: A. W. Swallows
Year Built: 1889 (R1973) (R1991)
Truss Type: Tied Arch
Dimensions: 1 Span, 37 Feet

Photo Tip: Easy all sides

Notes: A very simple looking windowless structure but have a look at the tied arch which is interesting

World Index Number: 45-14-10

National Register of Historic Places: July 2, 1973

Bower's Covered Bridge
(Brownsville Covered Bridge)

Township: West Windsor
County: Windsor

GPS Position: N 43° 27.662' W 72° 29.438'
Directions: From the town of Brownsville take VT-44 southwest for 1.3 miles, then right on Bible Hill Rd and right on Bowers Rd.

Crosses: Mill Brook
Carries: Bowers Road

Builder: Not known
Year Built: c1919 (R2001) (R2012)
Truss Type: Tied Arch
Dimensions: 1 Span, 45 Feet

Photo Tip: In 2012 the bridge was being rebuilt after damage to the abutments from Hurricane Irene. It looks in great shape after re-opening.
Notes: Uses the interesting Tied Arch

World Index Number: 45-14-11
National Register of Historic Places: August 28, 1973

Windsor-Cornish Covered Bridge

Township: Windsor (Vermont) Cornish (New Hampshire)
County: Windsor (Vermont) Sullivan (New Hampshire)

GPS Position: N 43° 28.375' W 72° 22.996'

Directions: From the town of Windsor, Vermont, take US-5/ VT-12/ Main St. south for 0.3 miles and turn left on Bridge St. From the town of Cornish, New Hampshire, take Mill Village Road and continue on Town House Road and NH-12 for 1.5 miles and the bridge will appear on your left.

Crosses: Connecticut River

Carries: Bridge Street (Vermont) Cornish Toll Road (New Hampshire)

Builder: James Tasker & Bela J. Fletcher
Year Built: 1866 (R1887) (R1892)(R1887) (R1925) (R1887) (R1938) (R1955) (R1977) (R1989) (R2001)
Truss Type: Town
Dimensions: 2 Span, 449 Feet, 2 Lanes

Photo Tip: There are good views from front and sides but watch for traffic. The new Hampshire side is a bit better
Notes: This is one of the finest covered bridges in North America with a toe in Vermont and the bulk in New Hampshire. It is the longest two span bridge in the world.

World Index Number: 45-14-14#2 (Vermont) 29-10-09#2 (New Hampshire)
National Register of Historic Places: November 21. 1976

Martinsville Covered Bridge
(Martin's Mill Covered Bridge)

Township: Hartland
County: Windsor

GPS Position: N 43° 31.955' W 72° 23.749'
Directions: From the town of Hartland, take Us-5 east and after 0.4 miles turn right on Depot Rd and then another quick right onto Martinsville Rd. The bridge site is about 0.7 miles.

Crosses: Lull's Brook
Carries: Martinsville Rd.

Builder: James F. Tasker
Year Built: 1881 (R1979)
Truss Type: Town
Dimensions: 1 Span, 135 Feet

Photo Tip: While not a particularly photogenic structure, it is easy to find clear set up areas.
Notes: The ruins of the old mill are near the bridge. The area is quiet now but once had a busy industrial operation.

World Index Number: 45-14-01
National Register of Historic Places: August 28, 1973

Willard Covered Bridge
(West Hartland Covered Bridge)

Township: Hartland
County: Windsor

GPS Position: N 43° 35.611' W 72° 20.973'
Directions: From the town of North Hartland take Ewarts Drive south off US-5 and take the first left on Mill St. The bridge is then a short distance.

Crosses: Ottauquechee River
Carries: Mill St.

Builder: Not Known
Year Built: 1870 (R1953) (R1979)
Truss Type: Town
Dimensions: 1 Span, 124 Feet

Photo Tip: It is easy to get a shot with both bridges in the frame. Side views are available with care.
Notes: The bridge originally was without windows which were added in the 1953 renovation. This was said to keep horses from being startled by the rough water below. Just west of this bridge is another called the Williard Twin Covered Bridge.

World Index Number: 45-14-02
National Register of Historic Places: August 28, 1973

Willard Twin Covered Bridge
(North Hartland Twin Covered Bridge)

Township: Hartland
County: Windsor

GPS Position: N 43° 35.611' W 72° 20.973'

Directions: From the town of North Hartland take Ewarts Drive south off US-5 and take the first left on Mill St. The bridge is then a short distance.

Crosses: Ottauquechee River
Carries: Mill St.

Builder: Not Known
Year Built: 2001
Truss Type: Town
Dimensions: 1 Span, 81 Feet

Photo Tip: It is easy to get a shot with both bridges in the frame. Side views are available with care.
Notes: The first bridge on this site was built in about 1872 and was destroyed in a hurricane in 1938. This bridge is an authentic replica completed in 2001 Just east of this bridge is another called the Williard Covered Bridge.

World Index Number: 45-14-64#2
National Register of Historic Places: Not listed

Baltimore Covered Bridge

Township: Springfield
County: Windsor

GPS Position: N 43° 16.240' W 72° 26.877'
Directions: From I-91, take exit 7,6 miles north of Rockingham, and continue on Charleston Rd./ VT-11 for 1.2 miles where you will see the bridge on your right.

Crosses: Unnamed creek
Carries: None

Builder: Granville Leland
Year Built: 1870 (M1970) (R1970)
Truss Type: Town
Dimensions: 1 Span, 45 feet

Photo Tip: There are good images available from three sides and in the fall, it is fronted by a colorful stand of sumac.
Notes: This bridge was relocated in 1970 and restored by Milton Grafton. It was formerly located in North Springfield over Great Brook. The historic Eureka Schoolhouse is beside it.

World **Index** Number: 45-00-00
National Register of Historic Places: Not listed

Upper Falls Covered Bridge
(Downer's Covered Bridge)

Township: Weathersfield
County: Windsor

GPS Position: N 43° 23.893' W 72° 31.337'
Directions: From the village of Greenbush, go south on VT-6 for 1.2 miles and turn right onto VT-131 and after 0.3 miles, turn left onto Upper Falls Road. The bridge is a sort distance.

Crosses: Black River
Carries: Upper Falls Road

Builder: James F. Tasker
Year Built: c1840 (R1976)
Truss Type: Town
Dimensions: 1 Span, 120 Feet

Photo Tip: Great views from all sides, including side views at river level.

Notes: The great looking stone abutments have concrete caps used to raise the structure during the 1976 renovation. Great place for a family visit and picnic.

World Index Number: 45-14-08
National Register of Historic Places: August 28, 1973

Salmond Covered Bridge
(Middle Covered Bridge)

Township: Weathersfield
County: Windsor

GPS Position: N 43° 25.626' W 72° 29.285'
Directions: From the town of Cavendish go northeast on VT-131 and after 9 miles, turn left on Henry Gould Rd. The bridge is a short distance along this road.

Crosses: Sherman Brook
Carries: Henry Gould Rd.

Builder: James F. Tasker
Year Built: c1875 (M1959) (M1986) (R1986) (R2002)
Truss Type: Multiple King
Dimensions: 1 Span, 53 Feet

Photo Tip: Easy from all sides and you can have a picnic.
Notes: This bridge was originally located near Stoughton Pond and crossed the Black River. It was moved when a reservoir was being built in that area and was used as a storage shed. In 1986 it was restored to use as a bridge when it was moved to its present site.

World Index Number: 45-14-05
National Register of Historic Places: Not listed

Titcomb Covered Bridge
(Stoughton Covered Bridge)

Township: Weathersfield
County: Windsor

GPS Position: N 43° 22.131' W 72° 31.056'

Directions: Found at the south end of the town of Perkinsville on Highway VT-106. It can be seen from the road in a field across from the Weathersfield Elementary School.

Crosses: Schoolhouse Brook
Carries: Private lane

Builder: James F. Taskar
Year Built: 1880 (M1959) (R1963)
Truss Type: Multiple Kingpost
Dimensions: 1 Span, 45 Feet

Photo Tip: Easy from all sides as the landowner allows visitors.
Notes: This bridge was originally located across the North Branch of the Black River in Perkinsville. It was moved to its present location due to the construction of a reservoir in 1950.

World Index Number: 45-14-04
National Register of Historic Places: Not listed

Middle Covered Bridge
(Union Street Covered Bridge)

Township: Woodstock
County: Windsor

GPS Position: N 43° 37.483' W 72° 31.233'
Directions: From the Village of Woodstock turn north on Union St off of US-4

Crosses: Ottauquechee River
Carries: Union St

Builder: Milton S. Grafton
Year Built: 1969 (R1976) (R1989)
Truss Type: Town
Dimensions: 1 Span, 139 Feet

Photo Tip: Portal views are easy but watch for traffic. No easy side views are available.
Notes: Found in the middle of the village, it has a pedestrian walkway as well as a lane for vehicles. It was arsoned in 1974 but the bridge was saved and repaired. Some of the arsonists had their wages seized to cover the repairs.

World Index Number: 45-14-15
National Register of Historic Places: Not listed

Lincoln Covered Bridge

Township: Woodstock
County: Windsor

GPS Position: N 43° 36.009' W 72° 34.139'
Directions: From the town of West Woodstock take US-4 southwest for 1.7 miles and

Crosses: Ottauquechee River
Carries: Fletcher Hill Road

Builder: R.W. & B.H. Pinney

Year Built: 1877
Truss Type: Pratt Truss with Arch
Dimensions: 1 Span, 136 Feet

Photo Tip: Open easy views from all sides
Notes: The Pratt Truss with an arch is an interesting combination, perhaps unique to this bridge.

World Index Number: 45-14-13
National Register of Historic Places: August 28, 1973

Taftsville Covered Bridge

Township: Woodstock
County: Windsor

GPS Position: N 43° 37.866' W 72° 28.058'
Directions: From the town of Taftsville, take River Road north off of US-4/VT-12 and the bridge is a short distance

Crosses: Ottauquechee River
Carries: River Road

Builder: Solomon Emmons III
Year Built: 1836 (R1869) (R1953) (R1960) (R1993) (R2002) (R2012)
Truss Type: Unique combination of Multiple Kingpost, Queenpost and Arches
Dimensions: 2 Span, 191 Feet

Photo Tip: From the west side there are excellent panoramic views from both sides which can include the dam
Notes: This is Vermont's third oldest bridge and it has a unique and interesting construction. In 2011 it was damaged by flooding from Hurricane Irene and in 2012 was undergoing repairs.

World Index Number: 45-14-12
National Register of Historic Places: August 28, 1973

South Pomfret Covered Bridge
(Smith Covered Bridge)

Township: Pomfret
County: Windsor

GPS Position: N 43° 39.732' W 72° 32.193'

Directions: From the village of South Pomfret, go east on Pomfret Road for about 0.2 miles

Crosses: Barnard Brook
Carries: Farm lane

Builder: Not known
Year Built: 1870 (M1973)
Truss Type: Town
Dimensions: 1 Span, 39 Feet

Photo Tip: It is on private property but can be photographed with a longer lens.
Notes: This bridge is half of an original bridge known as the Garfield Bridge located in Hyde Park in Lamoille County. It was spilt and moved to two locations by a developer. The other bridge, Twigg-Smith Covered Bridge, collapsed in 2002.

World Index Number: 45-14-18
National Register of Historic Places: Not listed

Self Guided Tours

Addison County Tour

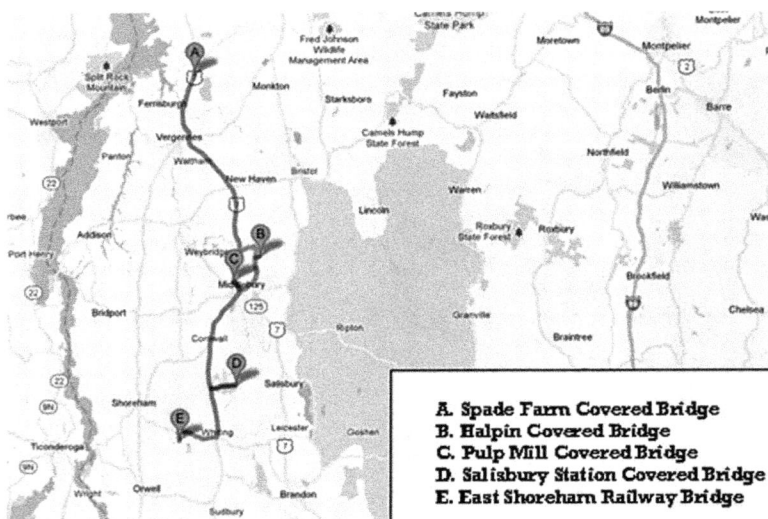

A. Spade Farm Covered Bridge
B. Halpin Covered Bridge
C. Pulp Mill Covered Bridge
D. Salisbury Station Covered Bridge
E. East Shoreham Railway Bridge

5 bridges-1 hour 18 min driving

While the Addison County tour includes only 5 bridges, they include a couple of the more interesting ones. We will travel from north to south.

We begin the tour at Spade Farm Covered Bridge. Its GPS position is N 44° 12.415' W 73° 14.885'. You will find Spade Farm Covered Bridge by travelling from the town of North Ferrisburg go west on Old Hollow Road and turn left on US-7 after 0.7 miles. The bridge is on the west side of the road after 1.3 miles.

This bridge was moved here in 1958 when a planned reservoir threatened its original location. The sign on the side indicates it was built in 1824 which would make it the oldest in the state but research indicates it was probably built in the 1850s. The interior contains some interesting things.

From Spade Farm Covered Bridge, we will head for Halpin Covered Bridge. You can set your GPS unit to N 44° 03.002' W 73° 08.459'

Head south on US-7 for 14.2 miles and turn left onto River Rd. After 1.0 mile take the 1st right onto Halpin Rd and continue for 0.8 miles where you take the 1st left onto Halpin Covered Bridge Rd. and the Halpin Covered Bridge is a short distance.

The Halpin Covered Bridge is the Vermont's highest covered bridge over its water course. It was initially built to access a marble quarry and the original abutments were made of marble.

Our next stop is Paper Mill (Pulp Mill) Covered Bridge. The GPS coordinates are N 44° 01.453' W 73° 10.663'.

Head west on Halpin Covered Bridge Rd toward Halpin Rd and after 0.3 miles, turn left onto Halpin Rd. Proceed for about 2.8 miles during which the road continues as Painter Rd., Washington St Exd., Seminary St, and finally Methodist Ln. Turn right onto Seymour St and after about 0.6 miles you will the bridge on Pulp Mill Bridge Road.

The Pulp Mill Covered Bridge is one of the few "double barrelled" bridges surviving in North America. Double barrelled refers to two lanes of traffic separated by a wooden barrier. Additionally this beautiful bridge has a pedestrian walkway.

From here we will head to the Salisbury Station Covered Bridge whose GPS position is N 43° 55.080' W 73° 10.445'.

Head east on Seymour St toward Seymour St Exd for 0.6 miles and turn left to stay on Seymour St. and after 0.5 miles turn right on Main St. Proceed 0.2 miles and at the traffic circle, continue straight onto VT-30 S/Main St. After 7.5 miles turn left onto Swamp Rd and the bridge is about 1.8 miles.

Salisbury Station Covered Bridge had a center pier added in 1969 but previous to that it's 155 foot span was the longest single span in Vermont. The name refers to a railway depot which used to be nearby.

Our final stop is one of the finest bridges there is. The East Shoreham Railway Bridge is at GPS coordinates N 43° 51.561' W 73° 15.363'.

Head west on Creek Rd/Swamp Rd toward VT-30 S/Seth Warner Memorial Hwy and continue to follow Swamp Rd. for 1.8 miles where you turn left onto VT-30 S/Seth Warner Memorial Hwy. After 3.5 miles turn right onto Shoreham Whiting Rd and then continue onto Richville Rd. Turn left onto Shoreham Depot Rd and after 0.7 miles you will see the parking lot for the East Shoreham Covered Bridge. The bridge is a short walk.

The East Shoreham Railway Bridge is a magnificent structure which has been kept in beautiful condition. There are less than a dozen covered railway bridges which have survived and this is one of the finest examples.

This ends our Addison County Tour

Bennington County Tour.

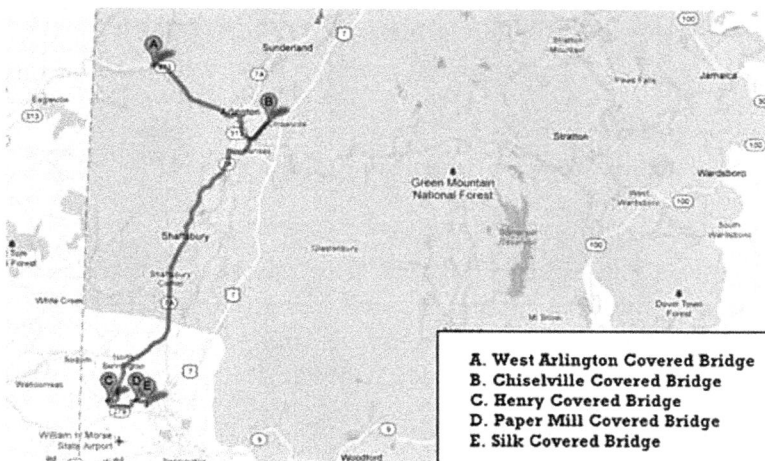

A. West Arlington Covered Bridge
B. Chiselville Covered Bridge
C. Henry Covered Bridge
D. Paper Mill Covered Bridge
E. Silk Covered Bridge

5 Bridges -Driving Time 43 minutes

The Bennington County Tour is a leisurely trip through some nice country.

We start our tour At West Arlington Covered Bridge, also known as Bridge At The Green. Its GPS position is N 43° 06.272' W 73° 13.208'.

From the town of West Arlington, the bridge is off VT-313/ Batten Kill Rd on Covered Bridge Rd.

The West Arlington Covered Bridge is at the entrance to the Norman Rockwell homestead and is a great place for a family outing.

From here we will head to the Chiselville Covered Bridge. Its GPS position is N 43° 04.345' W 73° 07.959'.

Head north on Covered Bridge Rd toward VT-313 E/Batten Kill Rd and in a short distance turn right onto VT-313 E/Batten Kill Rd and drive for 4.2 miles. Turn right onto Vermont 7A S/VT-313 E and after 0.2 miles take the 1st left onto E Arlington Rd and after 1.5 miles continue onto Sunderland Hl Rd where you will find the bridge. You can find an area to pull off past the bridge.

The Chiselville Covered Bridge is named after a Chisel factory which used to be in the area. Be careful if you are trying to get side views as the banks are steep.

Our next stop is the Henry Covered Bridge, the first of three bridges very close to each other. Its GPS coordinates are N 42° 54.737' W 73° 15.288'.

Head southwest on Sunderland Hl Rd toward Chiselville Rd and after 0.4 miles continue onto E Arlington Rd and then after another 0.7 miles turn left onto Warm Brook Rd. Drive 0.7 miles and turn right onto VT-313 W and then after 0.6 miles, turn left onto Vermont 7A S. Proceed for 8.2 miles where you turn right onto VT-67 W and go for an additional 2.0 miles. Turn left onto VT-67 W/Buckley Rd/Main St and continue to follow Main St, which becomes Water St. After 1.5 miles turn right onto River Rd/Water St and proceed for 0.7 miles where you will find the bridge.

The Henry Covered Bridge is a 1989 rebuild of the original 1840 bridge. The original bridge had doubled Town trusses but the current bridge has only single. This is a great looking bridge with barn red paint set off by white trim. It is easy to view and photograph from all sides.

Now we head to Paper Mill Covered Bridge whose GPS position is N 42° 54.737' W 73° 15.288'.

Head southwest on River Rd toward Ore Bed Rd and continue as River Rd turns slightly left and becomes Murphy Rd. The bridge is about 1.5 miles.

Paper Mill Covered Bridge was rebuilt in 2000 in an authentic manner after the original 1889 bridge was demolished in 1999 after being deemed unsafe. The new bridge looks excellent with its barn red paint.

Our last stop is the Silk Covered Bridge. Its GPS coordinates are N 42° 54.577' W 73° 13.519'.

Head northeast on Murphy Rd toward Vermont 67A S/N Bennington Rd and turn right onto Vermont 67A S/N Bennington Rd. After 0.4

miles turn right onto Silk Rd where you will find the bridge after a short distance.

The Silk Covered Bridge is another barn red bridge. It is one of the oldest in Vermont but has been maintained in beautiful condition.

This brings us to the end of our tour.

Caledonia County Tour

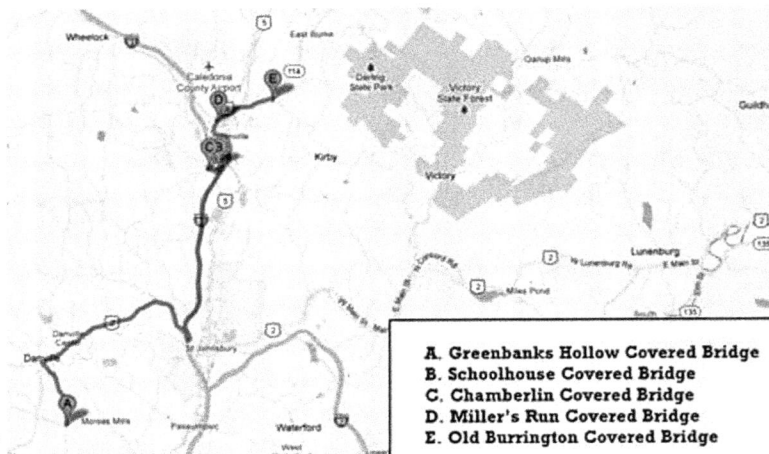

A. Greenbanks Hollow Covered Bridge
B. Schoolhouse Covered Bridge
C. Chamberlin Covered Bridge
D. Miller's Run Covered Bridge
E. Old Burrington Covered Bridge

5 Bridges - Driving Time 40 minutes

The Caledonia County Tour includes 5 Covered Bridges and driving time of 40 minutes. Our tour begins with Greenbanks Hollow Covered Bridge and the GPS position is N 44° 22.644' W 72° 07.328'.

To reach Greenbanks Hollow Covered Bridge from the town of Danville take Brainerd St. south from US-2 and continue on Greenbanks Hollow Road. You will find the bridge after 2.7 miles. If approaching from east of Danville, be careful that your GPS doesn't lead you astray on small roads.

Greenbanks Hollow Covered Bridge was originally built in 1886 but was rebuilt in 2002 when many non-authentic elements which had been added, were removed. It is a great looking bridge with a postcard look in its quiet country setting.

Our next stop is the Schoolhouse Covered Bridge whose GPS location is N 44° 30.977' W 72° 00.591'.

Head north on Greenbanks Hollow Rd toward Joes Brook Rd and continue on Brainerd St for 2.7 miles where you turn right onto US-2 E. After 6.9 miles, take the ramp to Newport onto I-91 North and go 6.6 miles to take exit 23 for US-5 toward State Route

114/Lyndonville/East Burke. After 0.3 miles turn left onto US-5 S/Memorial Dr and then take the 1st right onto South Wheelock Rd where you will find the bridge.

The small Schoolhouse Covered Bridge is found in a park-like setting which is quiet and natural. take a few minutes for some birdsong.

Now we head to Chamberlin Covered Bridge which is at GPS coordinates N 44° 30.963' W 72° 00.876'.
Head west on S Wheelock Rd toward Cross St and after 0.3 miles turn left onto Chamberlin Bridge Road. The bridge is a short distance.

The Chamberlin Covered Bridge which is also known as the Whitcomb Covered Bridge, is a nice open-sided bridge. Be careful where you park and walk as it occasionally gets some vehicle traffic.

from here we are heading to the Miller's Run or Bradley Covered Bridge whose GPS position is N 44° 32.533' W 72° 00.596'.
Head south on Chamberlain Bridge toward Acorn Ln and then turn left onto York St. and then after 0.3 miles a slight left onto US-5 N/Memorial Dr. Continue to follow US-5 North for 1.6 miles and turn left onto Center St. The bridge is about 0.5 miles.

The Miller's Run/Bradley Covered Bridge was restored in 1995 using some of the timbers from the original 1878 bridge. It looks excellent with white sides and pedestrian walkway. Watch for vehicle traffic.

Our last stop is the Randall or Old Burrington Covered Bridge. Its GPS coordinates are N 44° 33.198' W 71° 58.165'.

Head northeast on Center St toward VT-122 S/Stevens Loop and take the 1st right onto VT-122 S/Stevens Loop. Go 0.6 miles and continue onto VT-114 N/E Burke Rd. After 1.7 miles turn right onto Burrington Bridge Rd and the bridge is a short distance.

The Old Burrington Covered Bridge was bypassed years ago and in 2011, was not in very good condition. Photographers will love its beat up texture.

This is the end of our Caledonia County Tour.

Chittenden County Tour

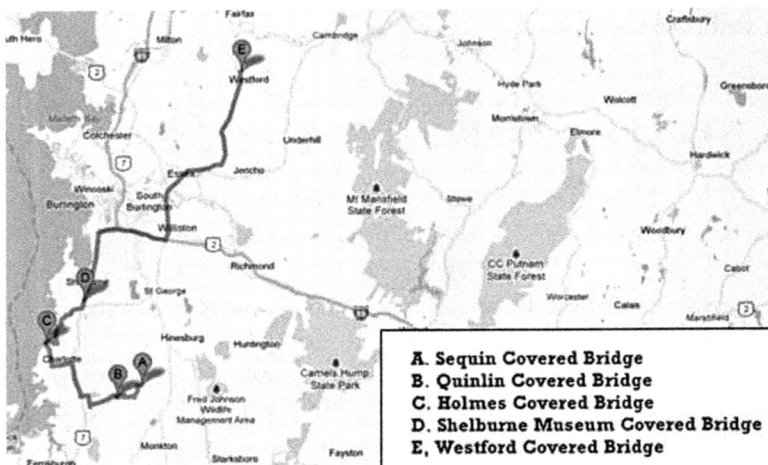

A. Sequin Covered Bridge
B. Quinlin Covered Bridge
C. Holmes Covered Bridge
D. Shelburne Museum Covered Bridge
E. Westford Covered Bridge

5 bridges- 1 Hour 23 minutes driving

The Chittenden County Tour includes 5 bridges and has a total driving time of 1 hour and 23 minutes.

We start at the Sequin Covered Bridge which is at GPS position N 44° 17.333' W 73° 09.002'. From the Village of Monkton Ridge go north on Monkton Road and take a slight right onto Silver St. After 0.4 miles turn left on Rotax Road and continue for 1.9 miles where you turn right on Roscoe Road. The bridge site is about 1.8 miles.

The Sequin Covered Bridge is in a quiet country setting although there are occasional vehicles so be careful.

Our next stop is the Quinlin Covered Bridge which is at GPS position N 44° 16.559' W 73° 11.047'.

Head south on Roscoe Rd toward Oak Hill Rd and after 1.1 miles turn right onto Lewis Creek Rd and drive 1.6 miles where you go right onto Monkton Rd. and as you reach Spear St., you will see the bridge.

The Quinlin Covered bridge is also in a quiet area and may remind you of the Sequin Covered bridge. The name of the builder of both bridges is unknown but may have been the same person.

Our next destination is the Holmes or Lakeshore Covered Bridge. Its GPS coordinates are N 44° 19.970' W 73° 16.940'.

Head northwest on Monkton Rd toward Spear St and continue straight onto Spear St for 2.1 miles where you make a sharp right onto Mt Philo Rd. After 0.9 miles take the 1st left onto State Park Rd and then after 0.6 miles, a right onto US-7 N/Ethan Allen Hwy. Go 2.5 miles and turn left onto Ferry Rd and after another 1.4 miles turn right onto Lake Rd. The bridge is about 1.8 miles.

The Holmes Covered Bridge is probably the lowest in elevation in Vermont and sits beside Lake Champlain. This is a popular area for swimming and family outings.

Our next stop is the Shelburne Museum or Cambridge Village Covered Bridge. Its GPS coordinates are N 44° 22.397' W 73° 13.859'.

Head northeast on Lake Rd toward Hills Point Rd for 0.9 miles and take the 2nd left onto Orchard Rd. After 1.3 miles turn right to stay on Orchard Rd and travel 0.3 miles where you turn left onto Bostwick Rd. Another 2.2 miles brings you to US-7 N/Shelburne Rd where you turn left. The bridge is found after 0.5 miles.

The Shelburne Museum houses the covered bridge which was moved here from Cambridge, Vermont in 1951. The museum has an admission charge but is worth a visit. The bridge can be viewed and photographed from the public road. The bridge has two lanes which were used for vehicles as well as a pedestrian walkway.

Our final stop is the Brown's River or Westford Covered Bridge. It is located at GPS position N 44° 36.748' W 73° 00.462'.

Head north on US-7 N/Shelburne Rd toward Church St and after 4.9 miles take a right onto the Interstate 189 ramp to Airport/Interstate 89 and merge onto I-189 East. After 1.1 miles, take the exit onto I-89 S toward Williston/Montpeller and proceed for 3.3 miles where you take exit 12 for Vermont 2A toward US-2/Williston/Essex Jct. In 0.2 miles turn left onto Vermont 2A N/St George Rd and continue to follow Vermont 2A North for 3.7 miles. Make a slight right onto VT-15 E/Main St and continue to follow VT-15 East for 3.1 miles. Continue onto VT-128 N/Browns River Rd for 8.2 miles and turn right onto Cambridge Rd where you will find the bridge after a short distance.

The Brown's River or Westford Covered Bridge was closed to traffic in 1965 after it was in danger of collapse. Funds were raised to restore it and it continues on a bypassed section of road.

This is the end of our Chittenden County Tour.

Connecticut River Tour

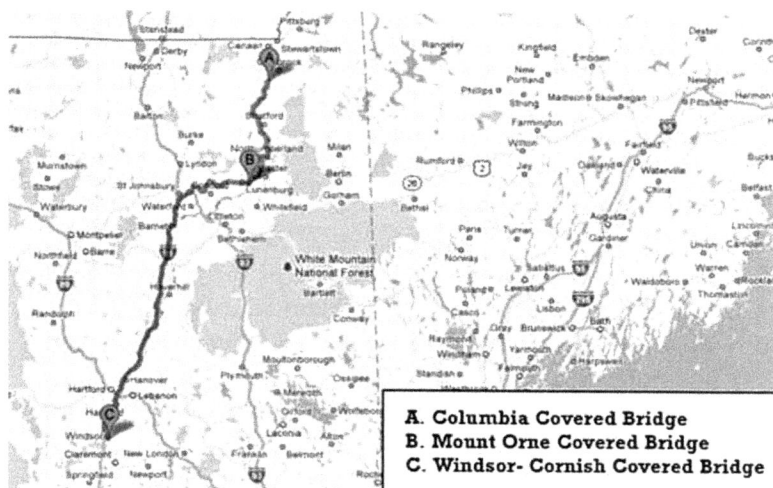

A. Columbia Covered Bridge
B. Mount Orne Covered Bridge
C. Windsor- Cornish Covered Bridge

3 bridges - 1 hour 42 minutes

There are three covered bridges which cross the Connecticut River which is the border for New Hampshire and Vermont.

We will start at the Columbia Covered Bridge which is at GPS position N 44° 51.159' W 71° 33.050'.Take Vermont-102 south from the Lemington area and turn left on Bridge St. The bridge is a short distance. From the New Hampshire side, take New Hampshire-26/ US-3 south from Columbia and turn right on the Columbia Bridge Rd. and follow a short way to the end.

The Columbia Covered Bridge was built in 1912, replacing a bridge which was destroyed by fire. It is the shortest of the three bridges at 146 feet as the river is still quite narrow here.

Our next stop is the Mount Orne Covered Bridge which is found at GPS position N 44° 27.634' W 71° 39.206'

Head northwest on Columbia Bridge Rd toward VT-102 S/River Rd and shortly turn left onto VT-102 S/River Rd, and continue to follow VT-102 South for 31.7 miles. Continue onto US-2 West for 3.9 miles and then make a slight left onto River Rd where you will find the bridge after 0.4 miles

The Mount Orne Covered Bridge was closed to traffic in 1983 but has recently re-opened after repairs. It is a beautiful structure said to produce a moaning sound in the right wind.

Our third bridge is the Cornish-Windsor Covered Bridge which is located at GPS coordinates N 43° 28.375' W 72° 22.996'.

Head north on River Rd toward US-2 W/E Main St and after 0.3 miles turn left onto US-2 W/E Main St and continue to follow US-2 West. After driving 20.0 miles turn left onto VT-18 south and in 0.4 miles, merge onto I-93 N via the ramp to U.S. 2. Drive 3.6 miles keep left at the fork, follow signs for I-91 S/White River Jct and merge onto I-91 south. Drive 68.0 miles and take exit 9 for US-5/VT-12 toward Hartland/Windsor. In 0.2 miles turn left onto US-5 S/VT-12 and in another 4.1 miles turn left onto Bridge St. where you will see the bridge.

The Cornish-Windsor Covered Bridge is one of the finest surviving covered bridge in North America. It is the longest two span bridges in the world. The New Hampshire side may offer the best views.

This is the end of our Connecticut River bridges tour.

Franklin County Tour

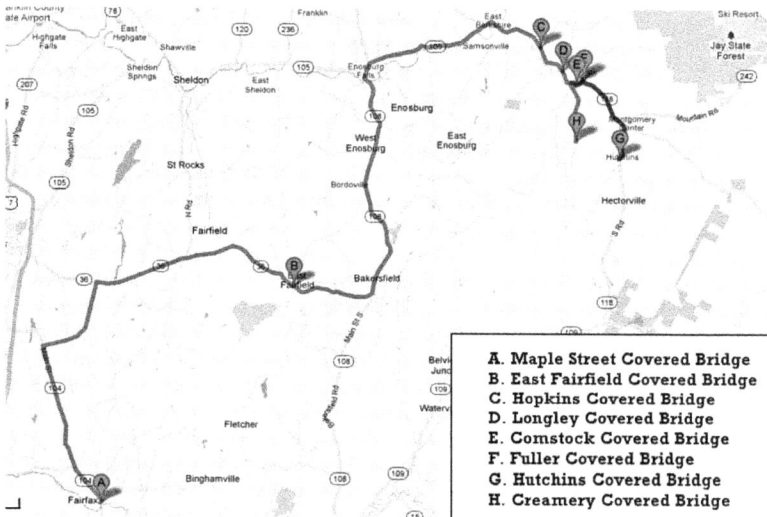

A. Maple Street Covered Bridge
B. East Fairfield Covered Bridge
C. Hopkins Covered Bridge
D. Longley Covered Bridge
E. Comstock Covered Bridge
F. Fuller Covered Bridge
G. Hutchins Covered Bridge
H. Creamery Covered Bridge

8 bridges - 1 hour 34 minutes

Our tour begins at the Maple Street Covered Bridge whose GPS position is N 44° 39.803' W 73° 00.630'.

In the town of Fairfax take Maple St south off VT-104/ Main St. and the bridge is about 0.2 miles.

Maple Street Covered Bridge, which is also known as the Village or Lower Covered Bridge, was washed downstream during the flood of 1927. If it looks to have a slight lean, it is because it was said to be restored with the east end facing west.

Our next stop is the East Fairfield Covered Bridge and its GPS position is N 44° 47.168' W 72° 51.719'

Head northeast on Maple St toward VT-104 N/Main St and turn left onto VT-104 N/Main St where you drive for 6.6 miles and turn right onto Brick Church Rd/Carroll Hill Rd. Drive for 1.3 miles and turn left onto Cadieux Rd and after 0.5 miles continue onto Swamp Rd. In 1.8 miles turn right onto VT-36 and proceed for 8.3 miles and turn right onto Bridge St. The bridge is a short distance.

East Fairfield Covered Bridge had extensive repairs done in 2009 and it is currently in beautiful condition. It carries vehicle traffic, so take care.

Our next stop is Hopkins Covered bridge. Its GPS coordinates are N 44° 55.229' W 72° 40.366'.

Head northeast on Bridge St toward VT-36 and turn right onto VT-36. Drive 3.2 miles and turn left onto VT-108 N/Main St North and continue for 9.2 miles when you turn right onto Main St. After 1.3 miles continue onto VT-105 E/Sampsonville Rd and VT-105 East. In 4.3 miles turn right onto Montgomery Rd/State Route 118 and after another 2.3 miles turn right onto Hopkins Bridge Rd. where you will see the bridge.

The Hopkins Covered Bridge was originally built in 1875 by Sheldon and Savannard Jewett who built a number of the bridges in this area. It was rebuilt in 1999 and looks in excellent shape.

Our next stop is the Longley Covered Bridge, only minutes away. Its GPS coordinates are N 44° 54.438' W 72° 39.333'.

Head northeast on Hopkins Bridge Rd toward Montgomery Rd/State Route 118 and after a short drive, turn right onto N Main St/State Route 118 where the bridge is a bit over a mile away.

The Longley Covered Bridge was also built by Sheldon and Savannard Jewett and it is found in a quiet setting. The weathered sides look great against the white portals.

Our nest destination, the Comstock Covered Bridge, is also close by. Its GPS coordinates are N 44° 53.969' W 72° 38.669'

Head southeast on N Main St/State Route 118 toward W Hill Rd and after 0.7 miles turn right onto Comstock Bridge Rd and the bridge is a short distance.

The Comstock Covered Bridge, also built by the Jewett brothers, offers some excellent open views. It also offers unpainted sides and white portals.

Next on our tour is the Fuller Covered Bridge whose GPS position is N 44° 54.199' W 72° 38.376'.

Head east on Comstock Bridge Rd toward Bank St and after 0.2 miles continue onto N Main St/State Route 118 and turn left onto S Richford Rd. After a quarter of a mile turn right onto Black Falls Rd where you will see the bridge.

The Fuller Covered Bridge is another Jewett brother creation. It has survived a few disasters including floods, truck damage and insect infestation and has come through looking good.

We will now head for the Hutchins Covered Bridge which is at GPS coordinates N 44° 51.520' W 72° 36.769'.

Head southwest on Black Falls Rd toward S Richford Rd and turn left onto S Richford Rd. continue onto Route 118. After 2.0 miles continue onto Main St/State Route 118 and after another 0.4 miles turn right onto Jay Mountain Rd/State Route 118. Continue to follow State Route 118 for 1.3 miles and turn right onto Hutchins Bridge Rd where you will see the bridge after a short distance.

The Hutchins Covered Bridge, also built by Sheldon and Savannard Jewett, is in a quiet setting although steel beams mar its appearance.

Our last stop is the West Hill or Creamery Covered Bridge built by the Jewett brothers in 1883, and whose GPS position is N 44° 52.069' W 72° 38.868'

Head northeast on Hutchins Bridge Rd toward S Brook Rd   and take the 1st left onto S Main St/State Route 118 and continue for 1.3 miles where you turn left onto Main St/State Route 118. After 2.9 miles turn left onto Hill West Rd and the bridge is a short distance. If it is winter the roads may be icy

The West Hill or Creamery Covered Bridge was closed to traffic for many years but a 2009 renovation has allowed it to re-open. Images from the side need care and you want to watch for traffic.

This is the end of our tour.

Lamoille County Tour

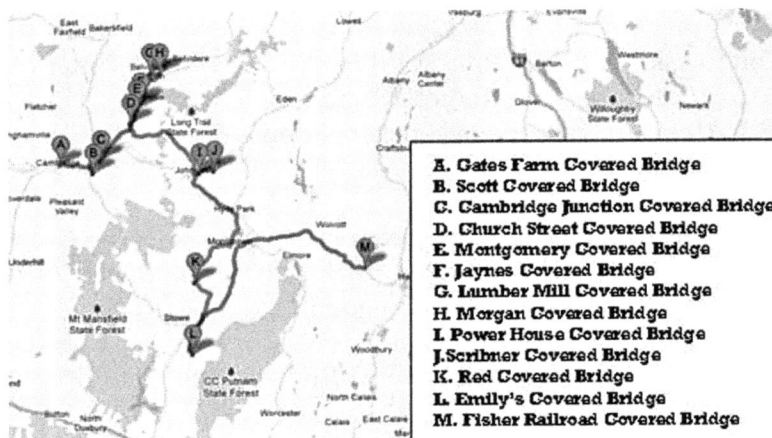

A. Gates Farm Covered Bridge
B. Scott Covered Bridge
C. Cambridge Junction Covered Bridge
D. Church Street Covered Bridge
E. Montgomery Covered Bridge
F. Jaynes Covered Bridge
G. Lumber Mill Covered Bridge
H. Morgan Covered Bridge
I. Power House Covered Bridge
J. Scribner Covered Bridge
K. Red Covered Bridge
L. Emily's Covered Bridge
M. Fisher Railroad Covered Bridge

13 Bridges - 2 hours 26 minutes driving

Our tour starts at Gates Farm Covered Bridge whose GPS coordinates are N 44° 38.741' W 72° 52.339'. To reach it, we start at the town of Cambridge and take VT-15 northeast for about 0.3 miles and we find the bridge on your right down a farm access road.

Gates Farm Covered Bridge was moved to its present location in 1950 and serves to access part of the Gates farm.

Our next stop is the Scott Covered Bridge. Its GPS coordinates are N 43° 02.930' W 72° 41.789'.

Head northeast on VT-15 E toward Pumpkin Harbor Rd for 0.2 miles and turn right onto VT-15 E/Pumpkin Harbor Rd, continuing on VT-15 East for 2.0 miles. Turn right onto Church St and continue onto Mill St and Canyon Rd for 1.1 miles where you will find the bridge.

The Scott Covered Bridge was built in 1870 and covered in 1873. Each of the spans has a different truss system and the Town truss portion is Vermont's longest covered bridge span.

The next destination is the Cambridge Junction Covered Bridge and its GPS position is N 44° 39.088' W 72° 48.798'.

Head west on Canyon Rd and take the 1st right onto Grist Mill Dr and continue onto Mill St. and Main St for 0.9 miles where you take the 3rd left to stay on Main St and then take the 1st right onto VT-15 East. After 0.7 miles turn left onto Cambridge Junction Rd and then take the 1st left to stay on Cambridge Junction Rd. The bridge is a short distance.

The Cambridge Junction Covered Bridge is currently closed and may not re-open. It is also known as the Poland Covered bridge names after Luke P. Poland, the former chief justice of the Vermont Supreme Court, who was instrumental in its construction.

The next stop is the Church Street Covered Bridge whose GPS location is N 44° 41.399' W 72° 46.262'.

Head north on Cambridge Junction Rd toward VT-109 and after 0.2 miles, continue onto VT-109 and drive 3.5 miles to Church Street where you turn left. The bridge is a short distance.

The Church Street Covered Bridge, also known as the Village Covered Bridge, has had run ins with a couple of trucks, the last of which caused its closing in 1999. It is easy to get to the rivers edge for excellent side views.

Our next destination is the Montgomery Covered Bridge found at GPS position N 44° 42.348' W 72° 45.616'.

Head east on Church St toward VT-109 and turn left onto VT-109 and after 1.3 miles, turn right onto Montgomery Rd where the bridge is a short distance.

The Montgomery Covered Bridge was built in 1887. It has excellent side views at river level.

Our next destination, Jaynes Covered Bridge, is only a short distance and its GPS coordinates are N 44° 42.719' W 72° 45.388'.

Head northwest on Montgomery Rd toward VT-109 and turn right onto VT-109. After 0.5 miles, take the 1st right onto Codding Hollow Rd and the bridge is a short distance.

Jaynes Covered Bridge, sometimes called Codding Hollow Covered Bridge, had a gravel truck drop through its deck in 1960 and has since been reinforced with steel beams. Side views have a lot of brush in the way.

We now head for Lumber Mill Covered Bridge at GPS coordinates N 44° 44.636' W 72° 44.476'. It is only a few minutes drive.

Head northwest on Codding Hollow Rd toward VT-109 continuing as it turns right. After 2.3 miles turn left onto Back Rd and the bridge is found after 0.5 miles.

The Lumber Mill Covered Bridge is located in a pleasant setting with good views from all sides. It has been fortified with steel beams and concrete piers after a 1971 encounter with a truck.

From here we head for the Morgan Covered Bridge, just two minutes drive. Its GPS position is N 44° 44.616' W 72° 43.684'.

Head northeast on Back Rd toward Florences Rd and after 0.7 miles take the 1st right onto Morgan Bridge Rd. The bridge is a short distance.

The Morgan Covered Bridge hasn't had steel beams added to it, unlike those nearby. It is found in a quiet setting with good riverside access, especially nice in the fall.

From here, we head to the Power House Covered Bridge whose GPS coordinates are N 44° 38.161' W 72° 40.198'.

Head southeast on Morgan Bridge Rd toward VT-109 and turn right. After 5.0 miles turn left onto Plot Rd and after another 6.2 miles, turn right onto Clay Hill Rd. Drive 0.9 miles and turn left onto School St. The bridge is found after 0.4 miles.

The Power House Covered Bridge, also known as the School Street Covered Bridge was re-built in 2002 after the original 1872 structure collapsed. It has steel beams added. Easy views and images available.

Our next stop is the Scribner Covered Bridge whose GPS coordinates are N 44° 38.383' W 72° 38.911'.

Head east on School St toward VT-100C, turn left and drive 1.1 miles and turn right onto Rocky Rd. After 0.3 miles turn right to stay on Rocky Rd and the bridge is a short distance.

The Scribner Covered Bridge started out as an uncovered bridge but was covered in about 1919. It is in a very quiet country setting.

Our next stop is the Red Covered Bridge which is located at GPS position N 44° 31.109' W 72° 40.669'

Head northeast on Rocky Rd toward Hunter Rd and take the 1st left to stay on Rocky Rd. After 0.3 miles turn left onto VT-100C South and drive for 1.4 miles where you turn left onto VT-15 E/Lower Main St East. Continue to follow VT-15 East for 4.1 miles and turn right onto Johnson Street Exd and then after 0.2 miles turn left onto Main St. In 0.3 miles make a slight right onto Depot St and continue on Cadys Falls Rd. In 1.4 miles turn right onto Stagecoach Rd and after a further 1.3 miles turn right onto Walton Rd. Stay on Walton for 0.8 miles and then make a slight left onto Cole Hill Rd. The bridge is on this road after about 3.9 miles.

Unlike a lot of red painted bridges which often have white portals or trim, the Red Covered Bridge's exterior is entirely red. It looks great in a natural setting.

Our next destination is Emily's Covered Bridge which is at GPS coordinates N 44° 26.422' W 72° 40.788'.

Head southwest on Cole Hill Rd toward Sterling Valley Rd and take the 1st left onto Sterling Valley Rd. After 1.6 miles turn right onto Stagecoach Rd and after another 1.7 miles turn left to stay on Stagecoach Rd and then turn right onto VT-100 S/Pucker St. Continue to follow VT-100 South for 1.6 miles and turn left onto School St and after 0.3 miles a slight right onto Stowe Hollow Rd. In 0.8 miles continue onto Covered Bridge Rd and the bridge is another 0.8 miles.

Our last stop is one of the most interesting bridges, the Fisher Railroad Covered Bridge. It is located at GPS N 44° 31.936' W 72° 25.660'.

Head northeast on Covered Bridge Rd toward Owls Head Ln and after 0.8 miles continue onto Stowe Hollow Rd and after another 0.8 miles continue onto School St. Drive 0.3 miles and turn right onto Route 100/VT-100 N/Main St and drive for 8.6 miles till you turn right onto Lower Main St. In 0.2 miles make a slight left onto Park St and shortly a slight left onto VT-15A E/Park St. In 1.7 miles turn right onto VT-15 East and after a further 8.1 miles, you will see the bridge.

The Fisher Railroad Covered Bridge is one of only two covered railroad bridges surviving in Vermont. It is a fabulous structure. Have a look at the cupola on top used to vent smoke from the railway engine.

This is the end of our tour.

Orange County Tour

A. Union Village CB
B. Thetford Center CB
C. Moxley CB
D. Braley CB
E. Gilford CB
F. Kingsbury CB
G. Howe CB
H. Ciley CB
I. Hayward CB
J. Larkin CB
K. Flint CB

11 Bridges - 1 hour 52 minutes

We start our tour at the Union Village Covered Bridge near the town of Thetford Hill. From the town, go south on Academy Road off VT-113 and the bridge is about 2.7 miles. It is at GPS position N 43° 47.321' W 72° 15.223'

Union Village Covered Bridge allows for some great open views and photographs. For the technical minded, have a look at the Multiple Kingpost trusses which have been supplemented by two long diagonals on each side.

Our next stop is the Thetford Center or Sayres Covered Bridge which is found at GPS coordinates N 43° 49.939' W 72° 15.149'.

Head east on Academy Rd toward Campbell Flat Rd and turn left to stay on Academy Rd. After 2.7 miles, turn left onto VT-113 W and then after 1.5 miles turn left onto Tucker Hill Rd. The bridge is about a quarter of a mile.

The Thetford Centre Covered Bridge has a concrete center pier that was added in 1963 to allow heavier traffic loads. The original covered bridges were normally built without windows although many had them added later.

From here we will head for the Moxley Covered Bridge whose GPS coordinates are N 43° 57.436' W 72° 27.816'.

Head northeast on Tucker Hill Rd toward VT-113 West and after 0.2 miles. turn left onto VT-113. Drive 18.7 miles and turn left onto VT-110 and then after 2.4 miles turn left onto Moxley Rd. The bridge is a short distance.

The Moxley Covered Bridge is located in a quiet natural setting. It is a fairly plain structure without windows and other adornments.

Our next stop is the Braley Covered Bridge which is located at GPS coordinates N 43° 55.704' W 72° 33.337'.

Head northwest on Moxley Rd toward VT-110 North and after a short distance turn right onto VT-110 North and after 0.3 miles, turn left onto E Randolph Rd. Drive for 3.3 miles and then continue onto Chelsea Rd for 3.5 miles. Turn left onto VT-14 South and proceed for 0.6 miles where you take the 3rd right onto Braley Covered Bridge Rd. The bridge is a short distance.

The Braley Covered Bridge started life in 1883 as an uncovered bridge. It was brought up to its present height and covered in 1904.

The next destination is the Gifford Covered Bridge whose GPS position is N 43° 54.977' W 72° 33.330'.

Head east on Braley Covered Bridge Rd toward VT-14 and shortly turn right onto VT-14 South and travel 0.8 miles and turn left onto Hyde Rd where you will find the bridge.

The Gifford Covered Bridge may also have started out as an uncovered bridge because it has an upper and lower level of trusses. It is painted a striking orange-red.

Next on our tour is the Kingsbury Covered Bridge whose GPS coordinates are N 43° 52.850' W 72° 34.903'.

Head west on Hyde Rd toward VT-14 and shortly turn left onto VT-14 South and after 2.9 miles turn right onto Kingsbury Rd where you will see the bridge.

The Kingsbury Covered Bridge is unpainted and looks excellent after a recent renewal. There is a bit of graffiti which is annoying.

The next destination is the Howe Covered Bridge. Its GPS position is N 43° 51.890' W 72° 29.901'.

Head east on Kingsbury Rd toward VT-14 South and turn right onto VT-14. After 8.0 miles turn left onto VT-110 North and after another 3.3 miles turn right onto Belknap Brook Rd where you will see the bridge.

The Howe Covered Bridge is also unpainted. Look for a homemade ladder hung on the inside wall.

We now head for Ciley Covered Bridge at GPS position N 43° 52.977' W 72° 30.256'.

Head west on Belknap Brook Rd toward VT-110 and turn right onto VT-110 North and after 1.2 miles turn left onto Howe Lane where you will see the bridge.

The Ciley Covered Bridge is unpainted and without windows, not untypical of the bridges in the area. It is in a quiet natural setting.

Our next stop is the Mill or Hayward Covered Bridge at GPS coordinates N 43° 53.485' W 72° 29.486'.

Head southeast on Howe Lane toward VT-110 and shortly turn left onto VT-110 North. In 0.8 miles, turn left onto Spring Rd where you will see the bridge.

The Hayward Covered Bridge is a newly constructed bridge which relocated an 1883 bridge lost in an ice jam. It has been built to authentic standards.

Next on our tour is the Larkin Covered Bridge which is at GPS position N 43° 55.381' W 72° 27.894'.

Head south on Spring Rd toward VT-110 and shortly turn left onto VT-110 North. After 2.8 miles turn right onto Larkin Rd and the bridge is a short distance.

The Larkin Covered Bridge is another simple structure without windows and unpainted but it is in a quiet rural setting and a nice place to visit.

Our last stop is the Flint Covered Bridge found at GPS position N 43° 56.956' W 72° 27.495'.

Head northwest on Larkin Rd toward VT-110 and shortly turn right onto VT-110 North. After 1.9 miles turn right onto Bicknell Hill Rd and you will see the bridge.

The Flint Covered Bridge is a very peaceful spot where you will see the oldest of the area bridges, built in 1874.

This is the end of our tour.

Orleans County Tour

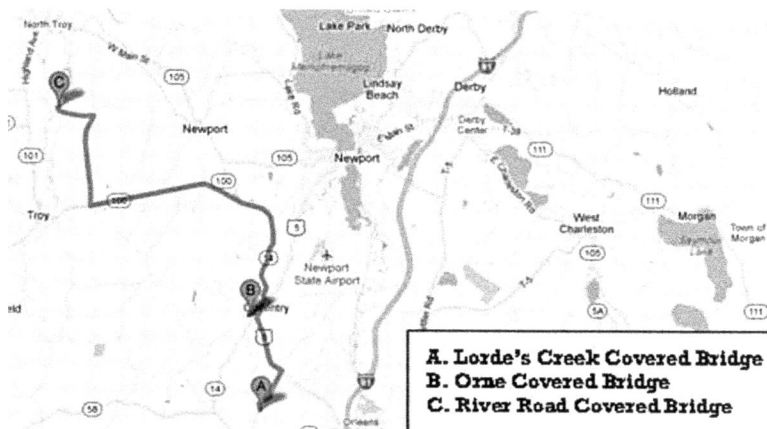

A. Lorde's Creek Covered Bridge
B. Orne Covered Bridge
C. River Road Covered Bridge

3 bridges - 25 minutes

We begin this tour at the Lord's Creek Covered Bridge which is found at GPS position N 44° 48.993' W 72° 15.971'From the town of Orleans, take VT-58 west for 2.7 miles and turn right onto Covered Bridge Road. The bridge is about 1.2 miles.

The Lord's Creek Covered Bridge is at the entrance to a farm access road after being moved here in 1958. It utilizes the rare Paddleford truss system, easily seen because of the uncovered sides.

Our next stop is the Orne Covered Bridge which is located at GPS coordinates N 44° 51.641' W 72° 16.444'.

Head north on Covered Bridge Rd toward Campbell Rd/T-20 and after 1.6 miles turn left onto US-5 north. Drive 2.3 miles and turn left onto Main St and then after 0.1 miles take the 1st left onto Heermanville Rd and shortly take the 1st left onto Covered Bridge Rd where you will find the bridge.

The Orne Covered Bridge   also uses a Paddleford Truss system. This bridge is an authentic replica of the original 1881 bridge which was arsoned in 1997. It is situated in a quiet natural setting.

Our last stop is the River Road or School Covered Bridge. It is located at GPS position N 44° 57.377' W 72° 23.694'.

Head northeast on Back Coventry Rd and after 0.2 miles continue onto Covered Bridge Rd. Drive 0.5 miles and turn right onto Main St and shortly take a left onto VT-14 north. Drive 4.8 miles and continue onto VT-100 south and then another 4.0 miles and turn right onto E Hill Rd. Continue for 2.9 miles and turn left onto Bergeron Rd and after a further 1.1 miles turn right onto River Rd. The bridge is a short distance.

The River Road Covered Bridge has interesting buttresses and is open on the sides near the top. It is in a nice rural setting.

This is the end of the Orleans County Tour.

Rutland County Tour

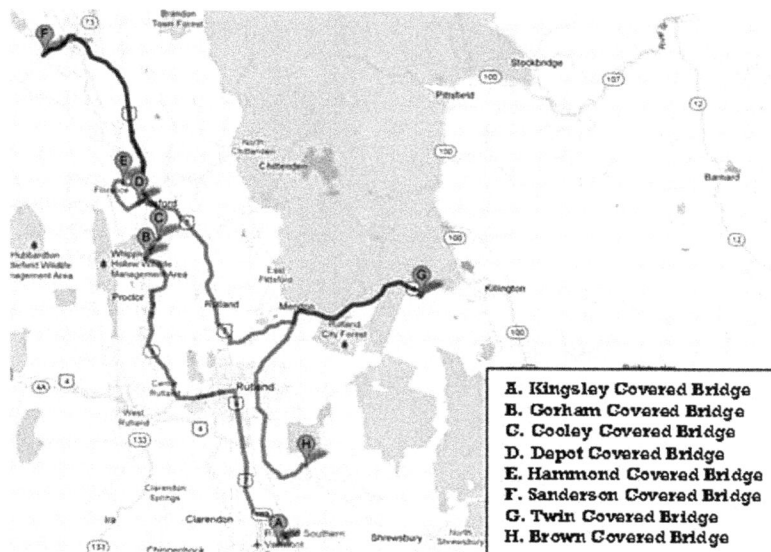

A. Kingsley Covered Bridge
B. Gorham Covered Bridge
C. Cooley Covered Bridge
D. Depot Covered Bridge
E. Hammond Covered Bridge
F. Sanderson Covered Bridge
G. Twin Covered Bridge
H. Brown Covered Bridge

8 Bridges - 2 Hours 19 minutes driving

The Rutland County Tour includes a number of bridges built by Nichols Montgomery Powers, considered by many to be one of the finest builders. Our tour begins at the Kingsley Covered Bridge which is at GPS position N 43° 31.418' W 72° 56.459'

From the Village of Cuttingsville take VT-103 northwest for 3.4 miles and turn left on Airport Rd, continuing on Gorge Rd/ River Rd. After 0.5 miles, turn left on East St. and the bridge is just ahead.

Found near the restored Kingsley Mill, it is one of the oldest bridges in North America if the 1836 build date is correct.

Our next stop is the Gorham Covered Bridge which is at GPS position N 43° 40.798' W 73° 02.237'.

Head north on East St toward Gorge Rd/River Rd and shortly turn right onto Gorge Rd/River Rd and then continue onto Airport Rd. After 0.4 miles turn left onto VT-103 north and drive another 1.8 miles where you turn right onto US-7 north. Drive for 4.8 miles and turn left onto US-4 BUS W/West Stand proceed for 2.1 miles where you turn right onto VT-3 north. In 5.9 miles turn left onto Gorham Bridge Rd and the bridge is about 0.5 miles.

The Gorham Covered Bridge is an authentic replacement of an 1842 bridge of whom the famous bridge builder Nichols Powers helped build. It is a great looking bridge in a nice natural setting.

Our next stop, the Cooley Covered Bridge, is close by and it is at GPS position N 43° 41.427' W 73° 01.691'.

Head east on Gorham Bridge Rd toward Elm St and shortly take the 1st left onto Elm St. The bridge is just under a mile away.

The Cooley Covered Bridge was built by Nichols Montgomery Powers and has been compared to a Conestoga Wagon. It is in beautiful shape after a 2004 update.

Our next bridge, the Depot Covered Bridge, is less than 10 minutes drive. It is at GPS coordinates N 43° 42.577' W 73° 02.557'.

Head east on Elm St toward Town Hill Rd and after 1.2 miles make a slight left onto US-7 N/Franklin St and then after 0.2 miles turn left onto Depot Hill Rd. The bridge is about 0.7 miles.

The Depot Covered Bridge is so named because of a railway station which used to be nearby. It is now a quiet setting and a pleasant place to visit.

Our next stop is the Hammond Covered Bridge whose GPS position is N 43° 43.238' W 73° 03.239'.

Head southwest on Depot Hill Rd toward Depot Rd and after 0.4 miles make a slight right onto Depot Rd and turn right onto W Creek Rd. After 1.3 mile turn right onto Kendall Hill Rd and the bridge is a short distance.

The Hammond Covered Bridge was one of many bridges effected by the great flood of 1927. It was washed downstream but floated back to its present position. It is presently closed to traffic.

We now head for the Sanderson Covered Bridge which is at GPS position N 43° 47.367' W 73° 06.686'.

Head southeast on Kendall Hill Rd toward US-7 S/Franklin St and after 0.7 miles turn left onto US-7 N/Franklin St and continue for 6.7 miles. Turn left onto Pearl St and the bridge is 1.3 miles.

The Sanderson Covered Bridge was a 2003 rebuild of the original 1840 bridge which used some of the original timbers and was completed in an authentic manner. It looks great and there is easy access from all sides.

We head next to the Twin Covered Bridge which is at GPS position N 43° 38.906' W 72° 58.319'.

Head east on Pearl St toward Martin Rd and after 1.3 miles turn right onto Conant Square and continue onto US-7 S/Center St. Drive 12.4 miles and turn left onto Prospect Hill Rd. Drive 0.7 miles and turn right to stay on Prospect Hill Rd and continue 0.4 miles onto E Pittsford Rd where you will see the bridge by the side of the road.

The Twin Covered Bridge is in a sad condition. The creation of one of the great bridge builders, Nichols Montgomery Powers, has been reduced to a graffiti covered storage shed. It is easy to view and photograph.

Our last stop is the Brown Covered Bridge which is at GPS coordinates N 43° 33.962' W 72° 55.107'.

Head west on Ox Land Dr toward E Pittsford Rd and shortly turn left onto E Pittsford Rd. After 0.8 miles continue onto US-7 south and after a further 3.3 miles turn left onto Cold River Rd. Continue on Cold River Road for 4.0 miles where you will see the bridge.

The Brown Covered Bridge was the last bridge built by Nichols Montgomery Powers when he was in his sixties. It is a great looking structure.

This is the end of our tour.

Washington County Tour

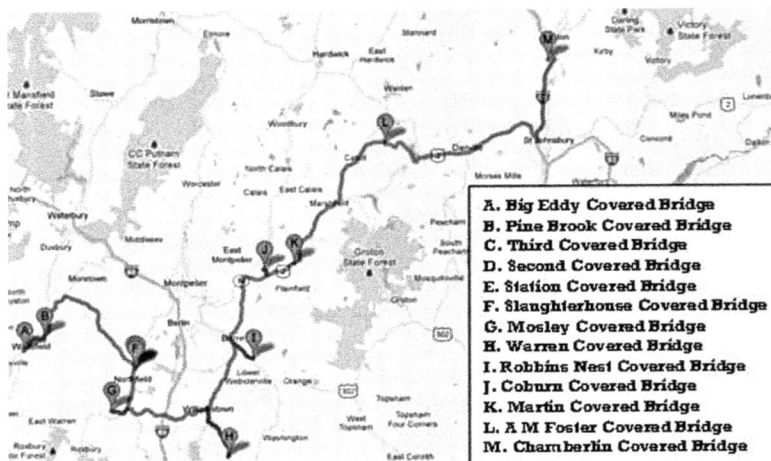

A. Big Eddy Covered Bridge
B. Pine Brook Covered Bridge
C. Third Covered Bridge
D. Second Covered Bridge
E. Station Covered Bridge
F. Slaughterhouse Covered Bridge
G. Mosley Covered Bridge
H. Warren Covered Bridge
I. Robbins Nest Covered Bridge
J. Coburn Covered Bridge
K. Martin Covered Bridge
L. A M Foster Covered Bridge
M. Chamberlin Covered Bridge

13 Bridges - 3 Hours driving

We start this tour at the Village or Big Eddy Covered Bridge which is at GPS position N 44° 11.362' W 72° 49.409'.

The Village Covered Bridge is found in the town of Waitsfield on Bridge St. just east of VT-100.Built in 1833, it is the 2nd oldest bridge in Vermont. You can get down to river level for good side views.

Our next stop is the Pine Brook Covered Bridge which is at GPS coordinates N 44° 12.339' W 72° 47.549'

Head northwest on Bridge St toward VT-100 N/Main St and take the 1st right onto VT-100 N/Main St. Travel 1.3 miles and turn right onto Trembly Rd and then after another 0.8 miles turn left onto North Rd. The bridge is about 0.2 miles.

The Pine Brook Covered Bridge, built in 1872, was renovated in 1977 by Milton Grafton, one of the last of the great bridge builders. It is in a quiet setting, especially nice in the fall.

We head now for the Third Covered Bridge whose GPS position is N 44° 10.425' W 72° 39.337'.

Head northeast on North Rd toward Bent Hill Rd and after 1.0 mile take the 1st left onto Meadow Rd and then after another 0.3 miles take the 1st left toward VT-100 N/Main St and then a sharp right onto VT-100 N/Main St. In 1.7 miles continue onto Vermont 100B N and then after 1.2 miles turn right onto Moretown Mountain Rd/Wimble's Rd and continue to follow Moretown Mountain Rd for 6.0 miles and then continue onto Cox Brook Rd for 2.4 miles where you will find the bridge.

The Third Covered Bridge is one of three bridges in a short stretch. It is a lovely small bridge.

Our next bridge is Second Covered Bridge, just a short distance, at GPS coordinates N 44° 10.366' W 72° 39.151'.

Head southeast on Cox Brook Rd toward Horse Lane and the bridge is only 0.2 miles.

The Second Covered Bridge is the middle of the three adjacent bridges. Like the other two, it is painted barn red.

From this bridge we can see the third of our adjacent bridges which is Station Covered Bridge. It is at GPS position N 44° 10.351' W 72° 39.084.

You can walk or drive to it. Just head about 500 feet east on Cox Brook Rd toward Chandler Rd.

The Station Covered Bridge is the third of our adjacent bridges and you can actually stand inside it and see the Second bridge through the portal. Be careful and look out for traffic.

Our next stop is the Slaughterhouse Covered Bridge which is close by. Its GPS position is N 44° 10.112' W 72° 39.268'.

Head southeast on Cox Brook Rd toward VT-12 South and shortly turn right onto VT-12 and after 0.3 miles take the 1st right onto Slaughterhouse Rd. The bridge is a short distance.

The Slaughterhouse Covered Bridge is similar to its nearby neighbors being barn red in color although its portal is rounded which is unusual. You can get to river level, which presents a fine side view.

Our next stop is the Mosley Covered Bridge whose GPS coordinates are N 44° 07.709' W 72° 41.775'

Head east on Slaughterhouse Rd toward VT-12 North and shortly turn right onto VT-12 S. After 2.4 miles turn right onto Vermont 12A South and a further 1.6 miles brings you to Stony Brook Rd where you turn right. The bridge is about 0.8 miles.

The Mosley Covered Bridge is a small bridge in a pleasant setting. The kingpost trusses are unusual in that they are only part height.

Next we travel to the Warren Covered Bridge which is at GPS position N 44° 06.672' W 72° 51.411'.

Head southeast on Stony Brook Rd toward Smith Hill Rd and after 0.8 miles turn left onto Vermont 12A North and after a further 0.7 miles turn right onto Lovers Ln and then continue onto VT-64 East. Drive 6.7 miles and turn right onto VT-14 S/Main St and in 1.1 miles turn left onto Chelsea Rd. In 2.9 miles make a slight right onto Stellar Rd and the bridge is about 0.6 miles.

The Warren Covered Bridge is in a pleasant setting. Have a look at the portals, one of which is straight while the other is on a slant.

Our next stop is the Robbins Nest Covered Bridge and it is at GPS position N 44° 10.735' W 72° 28.261'.

Head north on Stellar Rd toward Chelsea Rd at 0.6 miles and continue on Chelsea Rd for 2.9 miles where you turn right onto VT-14 N/Main St and travel for 6.9 miles. Turn right toward Washington St and follow Washington St for 1.2 miles where you continue onto E Barre Rd. You will find the bridge after 0.8 miles.

The Robbins Nest Covered Bridge is on private property but it beside the public road and easy to view and photograph but be careful of traffic.

Now we proceed to Coburn Covered Bridge which is at GPS coordinates N 44° 16.855' W 72° 27.233'.

Head west on E Barre Rd and after 0.8 miles continue onto Washington St for 1.2 miles. Make a slight right onto N Main St and in 0.5 miles turn right onto Maple Ave where you will travel for 0.4 miles and turn right onto VT-14 N/Maple Ave. Continue to follow VT-14 North for 4.7 miles and turn right onto US-2 E/VT-14 North. After 0.2 miles take the 1st right onto US-2 East and proceed 2.0 miles where you will turn left onto Coburn Rd. The bridge is about 0.6 miles.

The Coburn Covered Bridge is unpainted and the open top at the sides gives it a pleasant rustic look.

We now head for the Martin or Orton Farm Covered Bridge which is found at GPS position N 44° 17.255' W 72° 24.543'.

Head southeast on Coburn Rd toward US-2 East and after 0.6 miles take the 1st left onto US-2. The bridge is about 2.4 miles.

The Martin or Orton Farm Covered Bridge was obtained by the Town of Marshfield to cover a tax debt and it was moved to its present position in 2004. It has been nicely set up and easy to view and photograph.

We will now head for the AM Foster Covered Bridge which is at GPS coordinates N 44° 25.416' W 72° 16.042'.

Head northeast on US-2 E toward Onion River Rd and after 5.8 miles turn left onto Route 215/Cabot Rd and continue to follow Route 215 for 5.8 miles and then turn right onto Cabot Plains Rd. The bridge is about 1.6 miles.

The AM Foster Covered Bridge is in an open field on private property. You can see and photograph it from the road.

Our last stop is the Chamberlin Covered Bridge which can be located at GPS position N 44° 30.963' W 72° 00.876'.

Head south on Cabot Plains Rd and shortly take the 1st left to stay on Cabot Plains Rd and after 0.9 miles take the 1st left to stay on Cabot Plains Rd. In 0.6 miles continue onto W Shore Rd and in a further 2.0 miles turn left onto US-2 E/Theodore Roosevelt Hwy. Continue to follow US-2 East for 11.1 miles and take the ramp to Newport merging with I-91 North. Proceed for 6.6 miles and take exit 23 for US-5 toward State Route 114/Lyndonville/East Burke. Go 0.3 miles and turn left onto US-5 S/Memorial Dr. In 0.4 miles US-5 S/Memorial Dr turns slightly right and becomes York St. In 0.3 miles turn right onto Chamberlain Bridge Road where you will see the bridge.

The Chamberlin Covered Bridge can be busy with traffic, so be careful. This bridge has an interesting open construction.

This is the end of our tour.

Windham County Tour

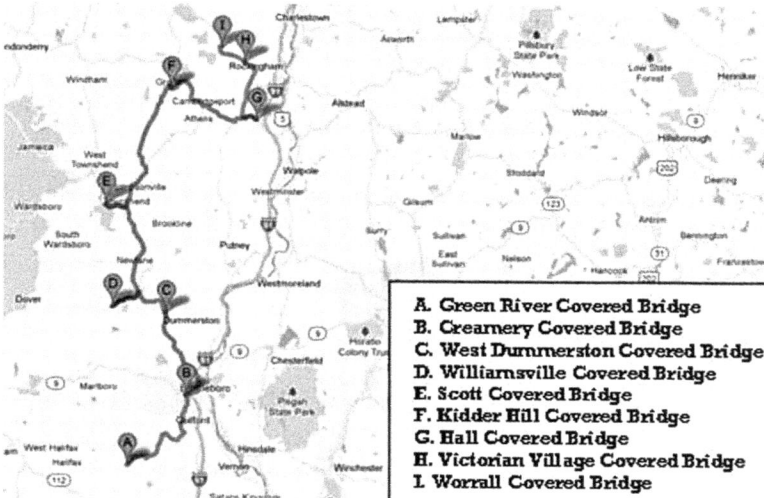

A. Green River Covered Bridge
B. Creamery Covered Bridge
C. West Dummerston Covered Bridge
D. Williamsville Covered Bridge
E. Scott Covered Bridge
F. Kidder Hill Covered Bridge
G. Hall Covered Bridge
H. Victorian Village Covered Bridge
I. Worrall Covered Bridge

9 bridges - 2 hours driving

Our tour begins at the Green River Covered Bridge. It is located at GPS position N 42° 46.531' W 72° 40.018'.

From I-91 just north of Guilford, take Exit 1 south on US-5 and go 1.4 miles where you turn right on Guilford Center Rd. After 4.6 miles turn right on Jacksonville Stage Rd and the bridge site is about 2.4 miles.

The Green River Covered Bridge is a great looking structure with its unpainted weathered sides offset by barn red portals. It formerly housed the mailboxes for the local people.

Our next stop is the Creamery Covered Bridge which is found at GPS position N 42° 51.012' W 72° 35.119'.

Head northeast on Jacksonville Stage Rd/Stage Rd toward Green River Rd. and after 2.4 miles turn left onto Guilford Center Rd and drive another 1.7 miles where you turn right to stay on Guilford Center Rd. Continue for 2.1 miles and turn left onto Tater Ln and then after 0.3 miles make a slight right onto Creamery Rd. Drive 1.1 miles and continue onto Guilford St and you will find the bridge in 1.7 miles.

The Creamery Covered Bridge has a pedestrian walkway as well as one for vehicles (although it is closed to traffic). It is an especially nice setting in fall.

Our next stop is my favorite Vermont bridge, the West Dummerston Covered Bridge. Its GPS coordinates are N 42° 56.170' W 72° 36.777'.

Head north on Guilford St toward Western Ave and turn right. Drive 0.9 miles and turn left onto Cedar St and after a further 0.7 miles turn left onto Linden St. In 0.5 miles continue onto VT-30 N/W River Rd and proceed for 5.8 miles where you will find West Dummerston Covered Bridge Road and the bridge.

The West Dummerston Covered Bridge is one of Vermont's finest and it is particularly spectacular in the fall. if you drive back in a upstream direction, you will find a couple of turn offs where there are exceptional long views.

We now head for Williamsville Covered Bridge which is at GPS position N 42° 56.653' W 72° 44.306'.

Head west on West Dummerston Covered Bridge and turn right onto VT-30 N/W River Rd. Continue to follow VT-30 North for 2.8 miles and turn left onto Grimes Hill Rd and after 1.6 miles continue onto Dover Rd. The bridge is found after 0.7 miles.

The Williamsville Covered Bridge is in a quiet setting and it is easy to make your way to river level for excellent side views.

Our next destination is the Scott Covered Bridge which is found at GPS position N 43° 02.930' W 72° 41.789'.

Head northeast on Dover Rd toward Baker Brook Rd and after 0.7 miles continue onto Grimes Hill Rd. In 1.6 miles turn left onto VT-30 N/Grimes Hill Rd and continue to follow VT-30 North for 8.5 miles where you will find the bridge.

The Scott Covered Bridge is an interesting structure as each of the three sections were built separately and if you look at the trusses you will see they are different. It is located in a beautiful setting.

The next stop is the Kidder Hill Covered Bridge which is located at GPS coordinates N 43° 10.119' W 72° 36.333'.

Head south on VT-30 S toward Stephenson Curve and after 1.6 miles turn left onto VT-35 N/Grafton Rd and in another 3.4 miles make a slight left onto Townshend Rd. In 1.0 miles continue onto Grafton Rd and drive for 5.5 miles where you turn right onto Pleasant St. In 0.2 miles turn right onto Kidder Hill Rd/Water St. and the bridge is a short distance.

The Kidder Hill Covered Bridge is in a quiet setting. Look for excellent river level side views.

Now we head for Hall Covered Bridge which is at GPS position N 43° 08.210' W 72° 29.267'.

Head northwest on Kidder Hill Rd/Water St toward Pleasant St and continue to follow Kidder Hill Rd for 0.2 miles and then make a sharp right onto VT-121 E/Main St and proceed for 3.9 miles where you turn left onto VT-121 E/Saxtons River Rd. Your destination is 4.4 miles.

The Hall Covered Bridge offers excellent side views which show off the diamond shaped windows. Located in a beautiful setting.

We now head for the Victorian Village Covered Bridge which is at GPS coordinates N 43° 11.680' W 72° 30.079'.

Head northwest on VT-121 W/Saxtons River Rd toward Hall Bridge Rd and in 1.1 miles turn right onto Pleasant St and after 0.4 miles continue onto Rockingham Hill Rd. Proceed 3.2 miles and turn left onto Meeting House Rd and after 500 feet, keep right at the fork. In 0.2 miles turn left onto VT-103 N/Rockingham Rd and the bridge is 0.8 miles.

The Victorian Village Covered Bridge is located on the property of the Vermont Country Store which is a very interesting place to spend some time. Look for the Grist Mill on the property as well.

Our last stop is the Worrall Covered Bridge which is found at GPS position N 43° 12.702' W 72° 32.127' This bridge was under repair in 2009 and suffered damage in 2011 from Hurricane Irene.

Head northwest toward VT-103 S/Rockingham Rd and shortly turn left onto VT-103 N/Rockingham Rd and proceed for 2.3 miles where you turn right onto Williams Rd. The bridge is only about 0.2 miles.

The Worrall Covered Bridge is the last stop on our tour.

Windsor County Tour

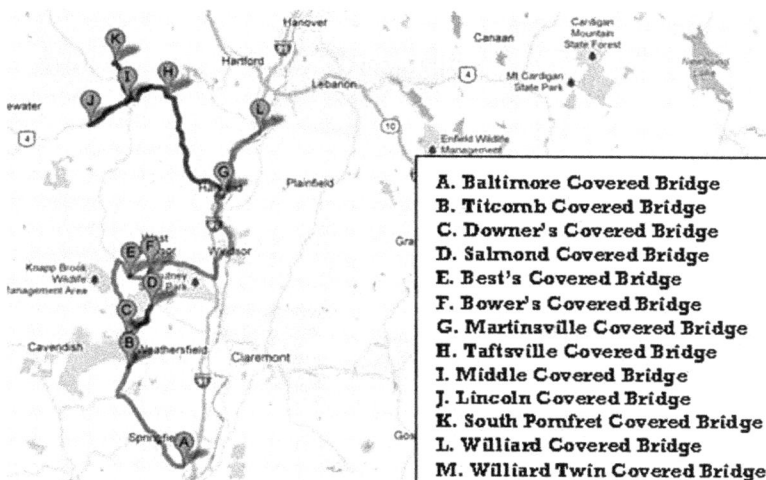

A. Baltimore Covered Bridge
B. Titcomb Covered Bridge
C. Downer's Covered Bridge
D. Salmond Covered Bridge
E. Best's Covered Bridge
F. Bower's Covered Bridge
G. Martinsville Covered Bridge
H. Taftsville Covered Bridge
I. Middle Covered Bridge
J. Lincoln Covered Bridge
K. South Pomfret Covered Bridge
L. Williard Covered Bridge
M. Williard Twin Covered Bridge

13 Bridges - 2 hours 30 minutes driving

Our Windsor County Tour begins at Baltimore Covered Bridge which is at GPS position N 43° 16.240' W 72° 26.877'.

From I-91, take exit 7,6 miles north of Rockingham, and continue on Charleston Rd./ VT-11 for 1.2 miles where you will see the bridge on your right. This bridge was restored by Milton Grafton after being moved here in 1970. In fall, the sumacs make it a colorful setting.

Our next stop is the Titcomb Covered Bridge which is found at GPS coordinates N 43° 22.131' W 72° 31.056'.

Head northwest on VT-11 W/Charlestown Rd toward Perley Gordon Rd and continue to follow VT-11 West for 2.6 miles where you turn right onto Main St. In another 0.3 miles continue onto VT-106 N/River St and follow it for 3.8 miles. The bridge is found after 2.2 miles.

The Titcomb Covered Bridge can be seen off in a field. Although it is private property, the landowner allows visitors.

Now we proceed to Downer's Covered Bridge which is located at GPS position N 43° 23.893' W 72° 31.337'.

Head north on VT-106 N toward Quarry Rd and after 2.6 miles turn left onto VT-131 West and in another 0.3 miles turn left onto Upper Falls Rd where you will see the bridge.

The Downer's Covered Bridge was raised in a 1976 renovation. You will find easy spots to view and photograph it from all sides.

Our next stop is the Salmond Covered Bridge which is at GPS position N 43° 25.626' W 72° 29.285'.

Head east on Upper Falls Rd toward VT-131 West and shortly turn right onto VT-131 East. Proceed 2.8 miles and turn left onto Henry Gould Rd where you will find the bridge.

The Salmond Covered Bridge has lived a varied life. It originally located near Stoughton Pond but was used as a storage shed after a reservoir flooded the area. In 1986 it was restored and moved to its present location. It is in a pleasant quiet location.

We will now head for the Best's Covered Bridge which is at GPS coordinates N 43° 27.300' W 72° 30.986'.

Head southwest on Henry Gould Rd toward VT-131 and shortly turn right onto VT-131 West and proceed for 1.8 miles where you turn right onto Amsden School Rd. After 0.4 miles make a slight right onto VT-106 North and drive for 4.5 miles and turn right onto VT-44 East. In 1.5 miles turn right onto Churchill Rd where you will see the bridge.

The Best's Covered Bridge is a short simple structure but the arch is interesting and worth a look.

Our next stop is Bower's Covered Bridge and it is only a couple of minutes away. It is found at GPS position N 43° 27.662' W 72° 29.438'.

Head northeast on Churchill Rd toward VT-44 and shortly make a slight right onto VT-44 East. After 1.5 miles turn left onto Bible Hill Rd and the bridge is a short distance.

The Bower's Covered Bridge was being rebuilt in the early part of 2012 after suffering damage from Hurricane Irene. It is in a quiet setting.

Now we head for Martins Mill Covered Bridge which is at GPS position N 43° 31.955' W 72° 23.749'.

Head south on Bible Hill Rd toward Bowers Rd for 0.3 miles and turn left onto VT-44 East. Proceed 6.8 miles and turn right onto VT-44 E/Union St. Go another 0.5 miles and turn left onto US-5 N/VT-12 N/Main St and continue to follow US-5 N/VT-12 North for 4.5 miles where you turn right onto Martinsville Rd. The bridge is about 0.5 miles.

The Martins Mill Covered Bridge is in a quiet spot which is easy to view the structure from all sides.

From here we head for Taftsville Covered Bridge. In early 2012 it was under repairs due to damage from Hurricane Irene although that is an interesting site. You may also find that some of the roads in our directions are closed. The GPS coordinates are N 43° 37.866' W 72° 28.058'.

Head southwest on Martinsville Rd and after 0.5 miles turn right onto US-5 N/VT-12 North and continue for 0.6 miles, then turn left to stay on VT-12 North and drive another 7.7 miles. Turn left onto US-4 W/VT-12 N/Woodstock Rd and in 0.5 miles, make a slight right onto Happy Valley Rd where the bridge is a short distance.

Built in 1836, the Taftsville Covered Bridge is one of the oldest in Vermont. It has a unique blend of truss types and a great place to visit.

We now head for the Middle Covered Bridge which is at GPS coordinates N 43° 37.483' W 72° 31.233'.

Head southeast on Happy Valley Rd toward US-4 W/VT-12 N/Woodstock Rd and shortly make a sharp right onto US-4 W/VT-12 N/Woodstock Rd. Drive for 2.8 miles and turn right onto US-4 W/VT-12 N/Pleasant St and follow it for 0.7 miles. Make a slight right onto Mountain Ave where you will find the bridge.

The Middle Covered Bridge is in the town of Woodstock and it attached walkway is busy with local use. The side views are not available and you need to watch for traffic but it is a great looking structure.

Now we will journey to Lincoln Covered Bridge which is at GPS position N 43° 36.009' W 72° 34.139'.

Head east on Mountain Ave and take the 1st right to stay on Mountain Ave and shortly turn right onto US-4 W/N Park St. Continue to follow US-4 West for 3.1 miles and turn left on Fletcher Hill Road where you will see the bridge.

The Lincoln Covered Bridge has an interesting Arch truss combined with a Pratt truss system, perhaps the only bridge of this design. You will find easy access to all sides.

Next we head for South Pomfret Covered Bridge which is at GPS coordinates N 43° 39.732' W 72° 32.193'.

Head north toward US-4 W/Woodstock Rd and shortly turn right onto US-4 E/Woodstock Rd and follow it east for 3.4 miles. make a sharp left onto VT-12 N/Pleasant St and after 0.2 miles turn right onto VT-12 N/Elm St. In another 0.2 miles turn right onto VT-12 North and go 0.9 miles where you make a slight right onto Pomfret Rd. In 1.8 miles you will see a farm lane on the left and the bridge is a short distance.

The South Pomfret Covered Bridge is on private property but is easy to view and photograph. It is half of the original bridge which was split and moved to separate locations.

Our final stop is a special one because it has two bridges, Williard and Williard Twin Covered Bridges which are at GPS position N 43° 35.611' W 72° 20.973'.

Head northeast toward Pomfret Rd and shortly turn right onto Pomfret Rd and drive 1.8 miles where you continue onto VT-12 S/Elm St for 0.9 miles and turn left onto VT-12 S/Elm St. In another 0.2 miles take the 1st left onto VT-12 S/Pleasant St and proceed for 0.6 miles where you turn left onto US-4 E/VT-12 S/Woodstock Rd.

Drive for 3.3 miles where you turn right onto VT-12 South. Proceed for 7.7 miles and continue onto US-5 North for another 4.5 miles. Make a slight right onto Mill St and in 0.5 miles you will reach the bridges.

The Williard and Williard Twin Covered Bridges are located in an interesting spot with fast water and old buildings. The original bridge was built in 1870 and the second, called Twin, was added in 2001 and built in an authentic manner.

The Windsor-Cornish Covered bridge is in Windsor County but is included in the Connecticut River Tour

This is the end of our tour.

Glossary

Abutment: The abutments are the bridge supports on each side bank. Usually they were originally constructed of stone but they have often been replaced or supplemented with concrete through the years.

Arch: A curved timber or timber set which is shaped in a curve and functions as a support of the bridge.

Bed timbers: Timbers between the abutment and the truss or bottom chord.

Brace or bracing: A diagonal timber or timber set used to support the trusses.

Bridge Deck: The roadway through the bridge.

Buttress: Wood or metal members on the exterior sides which connect the floor beams and the top of the truss. Used to keep the bridge structure from twisting under wind, water and snow loads.

Camber: A planned curve in the structure to compensate for the weight of the structure.

Chord: The horizontal members extending the length of the truss meant to carry the load to the abutments.

Dead load: The load of the weight of the bridge itself.

Deck: The pathway through the bridge used by pedestrians or vehicles.

Pier: Stone/concrete supports built in the stream bed to support the bridge

Portal: The bridge's entrances.

Post: The truss's vertical members.

Span: The bridge length measured between the abutments.

Treenails or trunnels: Pins or dowels turned from hardwood, driven into holes drilled into the members of the truss to hold them together. Also used in mortised joints.

Truss: The framework which carries the load of the bridge and distributes it to the abutments.

Trunnels

Trunnels or Tree Nails are wooden nails used to join members

Truss Types

A Truss is a system of ties and struts which are connected to act like a single beam to distribute and carry a load. In covered bridges, these Trusses carry the load to stone abutments at each side and perhaps piers in between. Following are the most common types of Trusses used in Covered Bridges.

Kingpost

Kingpost is the simplest form of Truss with two diagonal members on a bottom chord, often with a vertical post connecting to the diagonals. The multiple Kingpost involves a series of Kingposts symmetrical from the bridges center. This allows for a much longer span.

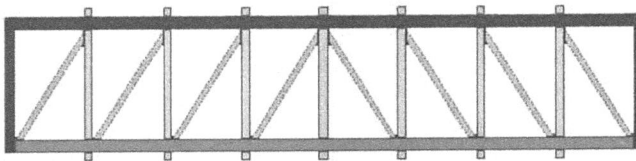

Multiple Kingpost

Queenpost

The Queenpost has the peak of the kingpost type replaced with a horizontal top chord which allows for a longer span.

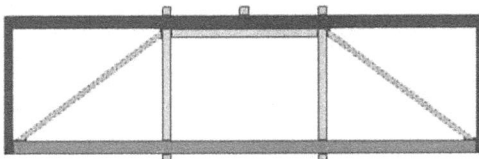

Queenpost

Long

The Long Truss was patented by Stephen Long in 1830. It is a series of X shaped diagonals connected to vertical posts.

Long

Burr Arch

Invented in 1804 by Theodore Burr, the Burr Arch is one of the most commonly found structures in Covered Bridge design. It is often used in combination with multiple kingposts. The ends of the arch are buried in the abutments.

Burr Arch

Howe

The Howe Truss was patented in 1840 by William Howe. It involves the use of vertical metal rods between the joints of wooden diagonals.

Howe

Town

The Town or lattice system was patented by Ithiel Town in 1820. It involved a system of overlapping diagonals in a lattice pattern connected at the intersection by Tree nails or trunnels, wooden pegs or dowels. It had the advantages in that it could be constructed by unskilled labor and local materials could be used.

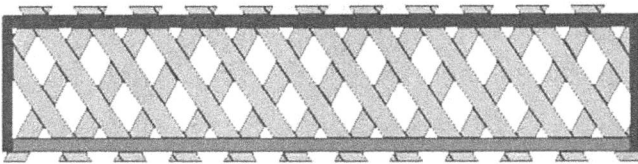

Town

Childs

The Childs Truss System is essentially a multiple kingpost with half of the diagonal timbers replaced with iron bars.

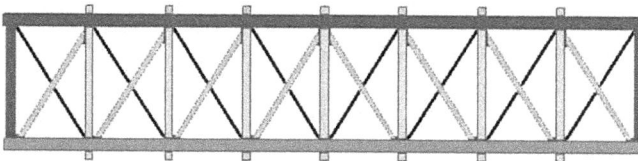

Childs

Pratt

The Pratt truss was patented in 1844 by Caleb Pratt and his son Thomas Willis Pratt. The design uses vertical members for compression and horizontal members to respond to tension.

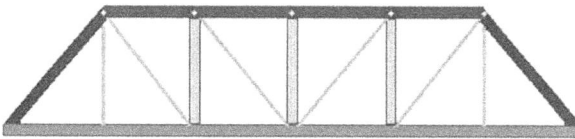

Pratt

Smith

Robert W. Smith received patents in 1867 and 1869 for variations of his system.

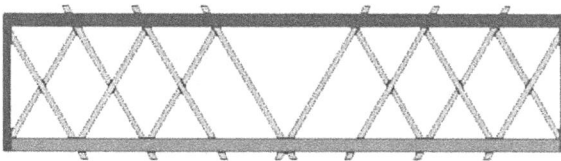

Smith

Partridge

Reuben L. Partridge received a patent for a design similar to the Smith system but adding terminal braces at the end and a central vertical member.

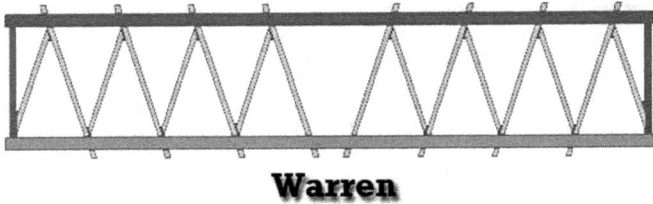

Warren

Warren

Patented in 1848 by two Englishmen, one of whom was named James Warren, it consists of parallel upper and lower chords with diagonal connecting members forming a series of equilateral triangles.

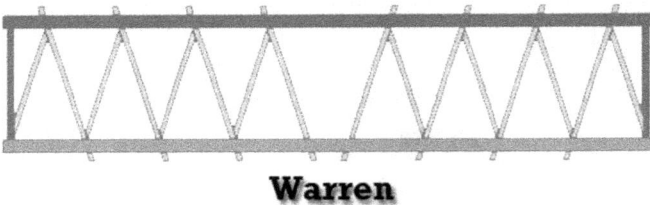

Warren

Paddleford

Peter Paddleford worked with the Long Truss system and eventually adapted it with a system of interlocking braces. he was never able to patent the system due to challenges from the owners of the Long Truss patent. However there are a number of New Hampshire and Vermont bridges which use the Paddleford system

Paddleford

Brown

Josiah Brown Jr., of Buffalo, New York, patented this system in 1857. It consists of diagonal cross compression members connected to horizontal top and bottom stringers and is known for economic use of materials. It was only used in Michigan where there are a couple of surviving members.

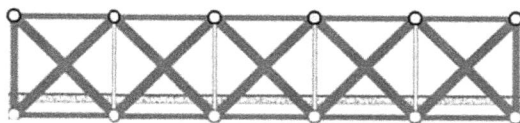

Brown

Index

www.ingramcontent.com/pod-product-compliance
Lightning Source LLC
Chambersburg PA
CBHW052001090426
42741CB00008B/1498